MEPHIBOSHETH!

Mephibosheth!: The Search for Identity, Purpose, and Community
Copyright © 2022 John Barnard

This book is set in the typeface Athelas designed by Veronika Burian and Jose Scaglione.

Cover art and interior design by Lawton Outlaw (lawtonoutlaw.com)
Cover photo by Michael Davello (michaeldavello.com)
Typesetting by Tall Pine Books

Paperback ISBN: 978-1-955546-31-7

A Publication of *Tall Pine Books*
119 E Center Street, Suite B4A | Warsaw, Indiana 46580
www.tallpinebooks.com

| 1 22 22 20 16 02 |

Published in the United States of America

MEPHIBOSHETH!

THE SEARCH FOR IDENTITY, PURPOSE, AND COMMUNITY

John Barnard

For Mandi

CONTENTS

FOREWORD

In the pages set before you, you will find a treasure chest full of rich thoughts and valuable truths. John Barnard writes with a style that engages your mind in vivid imagery and your heart in deep devotion. From the angles of his own life, he has been shaped by God's guiding hand to be a useful tool in building kingdom people.

From the streets, skate ramps, and concrete sidewalks of South Houston, John has a distinct perspective of life and ministry. God has created him with a quick-wit, sharp mind, and creative writing style that makes this book come alive. I have had a front row seat to God's creative work in his life and for that I am truly grateful. It is with a "misty eye" that I read his work and recognize God's grace, wisdom, and provision for John and his family.

With the story of David and Mephibosheth, John unpacks a life-lesson of redemption, grace, restoration, and promise. He finds small morsels of meaningful truth that can be applied to each of our lives. Identity. Purpose. Community.

All of these are explored with unique illustrations and perspectives that I believe will engage and inspire your mind and spirit.

It is my prayer that within the pages of this book you will find some truths of Scripture and life that will spark joy, laughter, introspection, or the need to sit with a close friend and eat a taco.

–Troy Sikes

WE ARE THE MUSIC MAKERS

(Introduction)

We are the music makers
and we are the dreamers of dreams,
Wandering by lone sea-breakers,
and sitting by desolate streams;—
World-losers and world-forsakers,
on whom the pale moon gleams:
Yet we are the movers and shakers
of the world for ever, it seems
-from Arthur O'Shaughnessy's "Ode"

The first lines of this poem are delivered in *the 1971 film, Willy Wonka and the Chocolate Factory*, when Gene Wilder's fantastic Wonka grabs the cheeks of the very cheeky Veruca Salt and calmly explains, "we are the music makers, and we are the dreamers of dreams." It would be natural to interpret Wonka's words to mean that after taking offense to Veruca's calling out his snozzberry nonsense, he chose to defend himself and those in his camp.

Isn't it part of our human condition that after being hurt by someone's negative or critical opinion of us or our value system, we fire back a statement of equal or increasing offense that serves to greater define a line in the sand between us?

Consider that perhaps Wonka wasn't clarifying his position in opposition to Veruca's. What if he was reminding her that, she too, has been fearfully and wonderfully made so the "we" that Wonka speaks of includes her as well; that she also is a music maker and a dreamer who has yet to hear the melody or allow herself the chance to consider building what has yet to exist. (She does, in fact, perform her own song moments later when revealing that she not only wants a feast, but she wants a bean feast.)

I have written this book with a similar approach in mind. I hope we can stack hands on some ideas whether I, as the writer, or you, as the reader, share opinions or value systems. That being said, if you find the following pages to be useless, just remember, "a little nonsense now and then is relished by the wisest man."

"Is This Art or Instruction?"

That was the question my friend, Craig, asked as I started to explain this book idea to him one day in my shop. My knee jerk response was (and continues to be) "I think it's both." The distinction between art and instruction (or creative expression and functional practicality) is a confusing one and has always felt very artificial. When I began teaching creative concepts at ministry conferences, I learned quickly that many ministry leaders carried with them a highly defined and rigid definition of their leadership style. While once sharing the concept of project-based mentoring with a group of pastors, a guy raised his hand toward the end of my presentation and asked, "but what if you're not a creative?" I asked him to expound on the term and tell me how what we were talking about could be affected if spearheaded or supported by someone who does not consider himself to be a "creative."

The pastor did well to explain the idea with more detail by describing church leaders who may be analytical and formulaic in their approach to ministry. These leaders struggle to think creatively or plan and design in a way that expresses artistic depth or originality.

Without getting too far into the weeds of personality types and psychology, I admit that some folks are simply news radio people instead of music lovers. These are the straight-forward ones that like numbers and stick to the literal meaning of things instead of nuance and metaphor. Maybe these people consider food to simply exist as necessary fuel for their bodies instead of understanding that a well-crafted taco can be nothing short of Paradise in a corn tortilla.

We rob ourselves and our world when we fail to see the creative in all things. After all, we have been creatively created by a creative Creator to join Him in the work of creative creation and re-creation. Read Genesis chapter one to see that each day was followed by a review and expression of contentment with that which was made. "And He saw that it was good..."

God created the cosmos with the beauty of design in mind AND ultimate practicality. He continually reinforces the process through adaptation and evolution. One doesn't get canceled by the other.

As I'll explain throughout this book, I get to head up a ministry called Middleman. It has always been a priority of Middleman Ministries that we set up shop at the intersection of Creativity and Productivity. By not remaining intentional about this, we risk operating from an imbalance in the approach. Working with skateboarders for so many years, we have met some very "creative" types who have many original ideas about art, music, and branding they want to produce. I have sat beside my fair share of young adults who enjoy smoking marijuana and sharing their ideas but have never done the work required to see their dreams take flight. They are very creative yet lack a productive nature or practice. (Maybe if I could get those very practically-minded conference attenders to connect with the skaters at the park, we could really get something going. Wonder Twins, ACTIVATE!)

Every day is a combination of art and instruction. Practical lessons get learned and relearned, yet not in opposition to beauty, but in step with it. There's metaphor everywhere. From the first moments of the morning, we reflect resurrection no matter our belief system. We are metaphorically brought back to life (or at least consciousness) as we open our eyes and rise from our slumber. By the time we tumble out of bed and stumble to the kitchen and pour ourselves a cup of ambition, we can already become joyfully aware of these monuments of grace that are piled everywhere. We may even be subtly reminded we should listen to some Dolly Parton on the drive to work today.

Whether our mindset is one so sharp that we can follow the words of Doug McKelvey within "Liturgy for the Ritual of Morning Coffee" as we drink the morning's cup...

Meet me, O Christ
in this stillness of morning.
Move me, O Spirit,
to quiet my heart.
Mend me, O Father,
from yesterday's harms.
From the discords of yesterday,
resurrect my peace.
From the discouragement of yesterday,
resurrect my hope.
From the weariness of yesterday,
resurrect my strength.
From the doubts of yesterday,
resurrect my faith.
From the wounds of yesterday,
resurrect my love.
Let me enter this new day,
aware of my need and awake to your grace,
O Lord.
Amen

...or we lack the motivation to do anything but endure the creaks and groans of our tired bones, aching muscles, or oppressed thoughts, even in this, we experience a blessed exchange of the old (yesterday) for the new (today). Maybe yesterday has left you with doubt or regret. Tasks you should have performed were left undone. Words spoken out of emotion and fear invade your mind and strive to find a second life in your resentful memories. Fight as you may to relive yesterday's moments, good or bad, they are gone for good.

Even in the shower, you symbolically wash away yesterday's defeats and regrets for the hope and preparedness of today. When you clothe yourself for the day with what most likely will be a clean outfit, you agree that there is a need to cover, protect, and make yourself presentable to a world, if even your small world, that needs to see, hear, and be blessed by you.

As you break your fast of the night, you reflect communion (this, of course, is the opportunity at every meal). Imagine being mindful that you are in constant need and that a meal prepared for you was grown or born from the earth, cultivated, tended to, reaped at just the right time, packaged, delivered, and prepared for you. Realizing just how many people it took for you to have that plate of Moons Over My Hammy placed before you at Denny's reminds us that every meal is ultimate communion and community in practice.

And when you begin interacting with your family, schoolmates, or coworkers? This is where the art is really shown in dynamic nuance and subtle obviousness. What if we could frame our public day within the context of jazz band performance? Your preparation (while already riddled with Gospel undertones) is merely running through scales. The real song is played throughout our day as we interact with our fellow musicians within the day's song. While we are studied well enough with our sheet music, we've sat in long enough to know the arrangement can change on a dime and that is where real life begins (and where we learn to stretch ourselves as musicians). The day will be full of give and take. The tension of living in the moment will wrestle with our mindless reach for our pocketed phones the instant we find ourselves standing in a line that doesn't seem to be moving.

And when the day's song is over? We feel the exhaustion of time well-spent making music with others, we settle in, turn out the lights, and rest because tomorrow is a new day and a new song. We, hopefully, feel a gratitude for the highs and lows, for those circumstances that we breezed through as well as the difficult ones that reminded us to lean in heavily on God and our neighbors' grace and mercy. We end the day as we started it, resigned to vulnerably lie back again and trust the sun will come out tomorrow. Because tomorrow is a new day, Lord willing and the creek don't rise.

Get On with It Already

As much as I hope you'll be equipped by this resource, I also hope you'll be encouraged. I see equipping as giving you a tool, like prayer or thoughtful perspective, and showing you ways and places it can be used. Encouragement is communicating the trust that you can do it, that I believe in you as one who was made in God's image. As a royal priest and household member, you have the power to exercise your faith in such a way that your children, mentees, or students will be blessed by you as you serve and lead them. You can do it because you matter and the daily work of one who invests in another is the hardest, noblest, most often underappreciated, yet essential, work of our time. If you find yourself neither equipped nor encouraged by the following chapters, yet you continue to trudge through this grammatical drivel, my hope is that you'll at least find something interesting to read about and that you're possibly inspired to YouTube a band or title of something you were previously unfamiliar with. A day spent learning something is a day well spent.

To each of you who, like David, after considering your many triumphs, resigned your heart to sit and ponder, "is there anyone left to show kindness to?"
I thank you

CHAPTER 1

SIT DOWN YOUNG STRANGER

(Mephibosheth!)

I'm standin' at the doorway
My head bowed in my hands
Not knowin' where to sit
Not knowin' where to stand
My father looms above me
For him there is no rest
My mother's arms enfold me
And hold me to her breast
They say you've been out wandrin'
They say you've travelled far
Sit down young stranger
And tell us who you are
-from Gordon Lightfoot's "Sit Down Young Stranger"

"MEPHIBOSHETH!"
They may as well have yelled it in unison as they pushed open the glass doors under the awning and made their way over to us sitting on the curb. Before they were halfway across the parking lot, we already started throwing Gatorade bottles and candy bar wrappers in backpacks.

"Yeah, we're leaving," somebody from our group yelled over his shoulder as we dropped boards on the ground to skate away. We could barely hear the "no, wait!" over the rumble of skateboard wheels as we pushed over the black asphalt toward the sidewalk running parallel to Broadway.

What I thought was happening on that day in 1987 was what always happened; we would ride over to a spot and spend as much time as we could manage before getting run off by annoyed business owners or chased by angry security guards. Few people outside the skateboarding culture understand that a twelve-year-old who loves skating bears a scarlet letter of sorts when he chooses to ride his board in the wild; outside the sterile barriers of a municipal-built and maintained homogeneous skate park.

It seems that for every well-intentioned church that hangs a basketball goal on a pole in their parking lot, they also hang a sign making it clear that loiterers, solicitors, and skateboarders are not welcome. But something was different about the deacons at Park Place Baptist who came over to the group of skaters enjoying the smooth concrete under the breezeway, the handrail, the concrete bench jutting out of the brick wall, and the grassy gap from said breezeway down to the parking lot below (my personal favorite).

Instead of telling us that the church doesn't have insurance and if we fell who would pay for it and can't we read because there's a sign right there that says our kind isn't welcome and that those marble benches were donated by a very wealthy family in the church, they told us something different. They told us that if we liked skating outside on the church property, we might want to go check out the gym floor inside the activity building as it's even smoother in there.

Instead of kicking us out, they invited us in.

I've had well over thirty years to remember that day. Even though I had no idea about what grace was at the time, I like that I experienced it in such a powerful way. Although I didn't realize it in the moment, these men communicated a deep theological truth to me by performing a simple act that included prioritizing liabilities.

I believe our daily lives are riddled with decisions determined by the ongoing measuring and comparison of liabilities. In the case of the Park Place parking lot in 1987, these men had to consider the fact that the easier decision, and one we often received, would have been to shoo us from the property while shaking a righteous fist and pointing to the sign on the wall with clinched teeth. Their decision would have satisfied the liability the church would assume had I and my unruly street rats/riffraff damaged ourselves and/or the marble benches in the prayer garden.

But thankfully, those guys realized there was a deeper and more significant liability to consider that day. The condition of my heart and soul were of greater consequence to them than the condition of the church property's parking blocks and handrails. While I would go on to learn about grace, mercy, redemption, sacrifice, patience, and true love once I began attending the church regularly, it was a gift to have these things shown to me long before they would be clearly explained to me.

Did the folks at Park Place Baptist know that the junior high skater they invited into the gym on a Wednesday night would go on to find his place in the youth group? That he'd respond to God's love for him by committing his life to the

Way of Christ? That he'd marry the music minister's beautiful daughter and have three incredible kids? That he'd defy the odds by moving out of South Houston and earn a degree from a state school followed by a masters? That his commitment to skateboarding would pay off in his becoming a sponsored skateboarder while in high school? Or that he'd spend over two decades shaping a career in church leadership before heeding the call to take a mentoring ministry full-time?

No, I don't think the decision to be hospitable that day carried with it any dramatic prophecy in the least. I just think, like King David from the Bible, these people were planted firmly enough in their identity and purpose to walk out in the Houston humidity, with cicadas chirping in the distance on Sims Bayou, and invite some skaters into their community.

While they may not have yelled "Mephibosheth!" to us that day, metaphorically, that's exactly what they were doing. The following account of the relationship between David and Jonathan's son explains the power of this name that perhaps you're unfamiliar with. By the end of this book, I hope you'll consider "yelling the name" into the hearts of all people God puts in your path.

The Man After God's Own Heart

The Bible describes David as a man after God's own heart (1 Samuel 13:14 and Acts 13:22). If you've ever read about his life, you know he steps onto the scene as a shepherd boy with a slingshot in his hand and a chip on his shoulder against anybody who has something bad to say about the God of Israel. You may also remember that he stole a man's wife after peeking in on her while she took a bath on a roof. David had a best friend named Jonathan but a tumultuous time raising sons. To investigate David's identity is to understand that he was a man with flaws who ultimately lived his life in pursuit of God.

David was the kind of man that wanted every experience that he could get. Think Bodhi from *Point Break* telling Johnny Utah: "If you want the ultimate, you've got to be willing to pay the ultimate price. It's not tragic to die doing what you love." (Man, I hope you were able to hear Patrick Swayze's voice there.) David wasn't satisfied by just hearing about something, he wanted to see it, feel it, and taste it. Much of the Psalms are written by him. Here are some words that describe David's character based on his written prayers to God:

Humble – Lowborn men are but a breath, the highborn are but a lie; if weighed on a balance, they are nothing; together they are only a breath. Psalm 62:9

Reverent – I call to the Lord, who is worthy of praise, and I am saved from my enemies. Psalm 18:3

Respectful – Be merciful to me, O Lord, for I am in distress; my eyes grow weak with sorrow, my soul and my body with grief. Psalm 31:9

Trusting – The LORD is my light and my salvation—whom shall I fear? The LORD is the stronghold of my life—of whom shall I be afraid? Psalm 27:1

Loving – I love you, O Lord, my strength. Psalm 18:1

Devoted – You have filled my heart with greater joy than when their grain and new wine abound. Psalm 4:7

Faithful – Surely goodness and love will follow me all the days of my life, and I will dwell in the house of the LORD forever. Psalm 23:6

Obedient – Give me understanding, and I will keep your law and obey it with all my heart. Psalm 119:34

Repentant – For the sake of your name, O Lord, forgive

my iniquity, though it is great. Psalm 25:11

Because God was at work on David's heart, he was able to express himself back to the Lord. We get a sense from Scripture that David was rarely confused about WHO he was and because he was confident in his identity, he was perfectly willing to react to those who insulted the very name of God.

1 Samuel 17 tells us what happened the first time we see David's story shared in Scripture. And what does his community ask him to do? Bring your older brothers their lunch! What are the fighting men of Israel doing? Sitting on their hands in fear of the large Philistine named Goliath. David was not having it. He asks those in charge what the warrior who takes this dude out gets. After they tell him, he tells Saul not to worry, he'll take care of it. Don't miss this. The next thing that happens is King Saul attempts to dress David in ill-fitting armor, *but David knows who he is*. He takes his familiar staff in one hand and his trusted slingshot in the other. David kills the giant with a rock and then, adding insult to deadly injury, he takes the uncircumcised Philistine's sword out of the giant's dead hand and cuts Goliath's head off with it.

The story continues with David standing in the King's court, catching his breath, and giving the account of what just happened outside. Oh, he was also holding Goliath's dripping extra-large sized head in his hand. Imagine the room as the story was being told. Everyone hanging on this young shepherd's every word. The confusion must have been palpable when considering what had just happened to this mighty foreign warrior by the hand of this – errand boy.

A nobody from nowhere.

But, like everyone else in the room, there was someone

there next to Saul listening to the play-by-play.

He had a much different take away.

The Other Man After God's Own Heart

King Saul's son Jonathan had already proven himself as a mighty warrior who had bravely defeated a garrison with only a steward at his side. David may have worn the moniker as a man after God's own heart, but we see every indication that Jonathan was also close to the Lord and was committed to living an obedient life no matter the cost.

Immediately following David's account of the killing of Goliath, scripture tells us that Saul began to fear David. The paranoid ruler would struggle for years to cope with David's popularity and success. Jonathan, on the other hand, was a "seated soul" who instantly recognized David as much more than a brazen shepherd boy, eighth in line of a lowly shepherd's inheritance. No, when Jonathan listened to David recount the courageous story of his killing the giant, he knew he wasn't meeting a cocky shepherd punching above his weight. He was meeting the next ruler of Israel.

In a symbolic display of selflessness that directly echoes what Jesus Christ did for mankind, Jonathan steps off his throne, places his IDENTITY onto David in the form of his royal robe and tested sword, and makes a covenant with David (1 Samuel 18:3). Jonathan reveals a seasoned maturity and sensitivity to God when instead of feeling self-righteous and threatened by David, he recognizes him as the rightful king.

We know Jonathan was a seated soul because he distinguished between the temporal and the eternal. Based on this distinction, Jonathan chose that which lasts forever by sacrificing what doesn't. If Jonathan's reaction to David's success was one of jealousy, he would have immediately felt resentment towards him and would have devised a plan to either downplay David's courage or work to harm him in some way. But Jonathan was confident in who God was and was secure in his own identity. Had Jonathan found his ultimate identity as the heir to the throne of Israel, he would have seen David as nothing more than a threat to it. Consider that while David was retelling the events of Goliath's death, Jonathan began to see David as the man who would be the next King. That is why we see Jonathan submit his very identity as royalty to David. It was an identity he was willing to give away as much as it was David's to receive and ultimately an act of obedience to God.

In 1 Samuel 20:15, after Jonathan commits to keeping David safe from Saul, he asks him to "not cut off your steadfast love from my house forever, when the Lord cuts off every one of the enemies of David from the face of the earth."

"Then Jonathan said to David, 'Go in peace, because we have sworn both of us in the name of the Lord saying, 'The Lord shall be between me and you, and between my offspring, and your offspring, forever'".

Scripture tells us later that Jonathan lived out the rest of his days fighting by his father Saul's side and that he met his demise on the battlefield with Saul and his brothers against the Philistines at Mt. Gilboa.

David would later honor his brother in arms by writing a song recorded in 2 Samuel 1 in which he sings, "Saul and Jonathan, beloved and lovely! In life and in death they were not divided; they were swifter than eagles, they were stronger than lions." (I can't find the beat either, but I'm guessing the lyrics rhymed in his native tongue.)

David Can't Lose

Let's pick this back up with a retelling of David's success in war. While Saul was a successful wartime leader, David prospered through all endeavors as the Bible tells us "The Lord was with Him."

2 Samuel Chapter 8 is a retelling of David's unique accomplishments on the battlefield. He was shrewd. He was strategic. He not only destroyed the forces against him, he also wisely turned his enemies' resources against them as assets for the advancement of his kingdom. Once the Philistines were destroyed, he moved onto the Moabites. He struck down two thirds of their army and kept a third to transform into his fighting force. David hamstrung most enemy horses but left enough to fortify his cavalry. He placed garrisons in strategic zones to maximize his influence and reign in foreign lands. David even took the plunder of valuable metals once committed to lifeless idols and redeemed them by dedicating them back to the Lord.

The chapter mentions that David's reign over all of Israel was characterized by justice and equity to all Israelites. It concludes with listing David's trusted men including his army commander, his recorder, the priests, the secretary, foreign affair representatives, and his sons as members of the priesthood. What a far cry difference from Saul! The paranoid war-time leader trusted no one and even threw spears at Jonathan when he defended his friend against the haunted man who suffered the presence of God leaving him after he so greatly confused obedience and sacrifice.

Saul is a reminder that the mark of a person's life will often be determined by the quality of people she surrounds herself with.

While 2 Samuel 9 is where we see David's IDENTITY shine, the chapter before it is a list of David's victories. To set this in modern terms would be to say that David spent his career winning everything. He won an Oscar, a Tony, an Emmy, a Grammy, the World Cup, the Super Bowl, the National Championship, the Winston Cup, all the gold medals, the Nobel Peace Prize, and the Kentucky Derby.

The most astonishing part of this is not the reality that David was a winner. We already know that because God blessed David with unparalleled success. We get it. Just like Parker Lewis, David couldn't lose. Let's focus on the result of this life of victory and the question that David asks of his court while sitting on his throne one day...

Kindness

Having just revisited all his incredible victories, does David ask for the royal mirror so that he may gaze upon his ruddiness with admiration? Does he ask the court musicians to write a song heralding his bravery? Does he commission a sculpture in his likeness to celebrate his chiseled physique?

He doesn't do any of these things.

Instead, he poses a ridiculous question. He asks if anyone in the room knows if there is anybody left in Jonathan's household that he can show kindness to.

The most victorious and cunning and strategic and capable of all of Israel's kings sits at the apex of his reign and the next question he asks is about the chance to show kindness to a stranger? I can hear point guard, Allen Iverson right now after being asked about practice – "Kindness. Kindness! Kindness? We talkin' about kindness?!"

That, my friends, is the greatest indicator we can find

about the true character of a man. So often we confuse pompous masculinity with the rightful destination of holistic manliness. The excellent example of King David shows such a vastly different picture. It's one that some men feel uncomfortable really looking into (and for that reason we will do just that). Take whatever translation you wish but spend some time looking at the deep brotherhood we see between David and Jonathan. These two young men loved each other as they loved themselves. David goes so far as to mention that his love for Jonathan was more valuable to him than his love for a woman.

The covenant that David and Jonathan made between each other was binding. And once his faithful friend died, David upheld the oath he made to protect and preserve Jonathan's lineage for the rest of his life.

So, of course, David asks the question to his royal court.

I imagine there was silence in the room for a beat or two, perhaps some shuffling of sandals. This is certainly not the first time David has done or said something that took people by surprise. Once, David danced before the Ark of the Covenant parade in (arguably) his underwear and his wife thought it was most unbecoming of a king to do so. But, again, David was more concerned with sucking the marrow out of life than worried about mildly offensive table manners. Maybe we take a page from David's book every now and then to remember that often in life it is not profession, preference, or presumption that defines us but, rather, we define them!

In the timeless words of modern theologian, Nacho Libre, "*anyways*," to David's great pleasure, a member of his court stops side eyeing and smirking with the guys next to him long enough to clear his throat and reply, "Well, yes there is. Jonathan has a son. *He is lame in both feet*." These were the words of a man named Ziba, who had previously served within Saul's household. But take note, Ziba shared an important piece of information by how he answered this question. It is remarkable that Ziba shows us how the world viewed this son of Jonathan, this man of royal blood.

Before we know this man's name, his *identity* is revealed to us as a man who is damaged goods.

Throughout history, a person's physical characteristics have directly reflected that person's worth to society. Think for a moment of the importance of large families in Scripture. Barren women are regarded as cursed while men with many children (especially boys) are regarded as blessed. Large families mean that the father has many workers to manage property and livestock. The fact this son of Jonathan is identified as lame reveals he is irrelevant and unworthy. Unworthy of even having his name spoken, or even remembered, in David's royal court.

King David asked about the whereabouts of the man.

The answer? "He is at the house of Makir, son of Ammiel, in Lo Debar." Ziba's answer uncovers another layer of irrelevance when considering a life spent in obscurity. For all matters of practicality, Makir, son of Ammiel, is considered a friend of the family who took Jonathan's son in after taking pity on him. The alternative was to leave him for dead as he would have struggled to take care of himself. Lo Debar's geographical location was akin to the man living in a one-horse town far from the mighty Jerusalem.

To recap, this son of Jonathan had been spending at least a decade of his pitiful life as a charity case within a borrowed room at a sympathetic business partner of his grandfather's in a town that nobody cared about and where nothing was happening.

A nobody from nowhere.

But still, David sends for him.

Next, we're told that Mephibosheth enters the king's court.

But wait a second. Let's consider this name as we know how often they are important in Scripture. Mephibosheth is a Hebrew name meaning "the end of shame." Yet we can only imagine that the bulk of this man's life has been marked by shame, inability, and being shunned. While life in Lo Debar was certainly uneventful and boring, it must have also felt safe for Mephibosheth. Imagine the young man's dread when David's officers knocked on the door, scooped him up, and loaded him onto a chariot headed straight for the palace.

Why would Mephibosheth fear for his life? It was common practice at this time in history for entire households of royalty to be executed when one king overthrew another. The reason for this is simple since to snuff out a preceding king's family leaves no one who can take time to gain political or military strength and come back to seek vengeance. When King Saul died on his own sword at Mt. Gilboa, his household made haste immediately to escape to safety. The Bible says that a nurse scooped up the boy of five but then haphazardly dropped young Mephibosheth causing injury to his legs and thus determined his destiny of hiding in Lo Debar. This is, of course, until David asks his question and changes Mephibosheth's story.

So, the world sees the young man with the disability as a liability.

But David's first word spoken to the young man?

"MEPHIBOSHETH!"

"THE END OF SHAME"

"SHAME NO LONGER DEFINES YOU"

"Yesterday you were defined by the things you lacked. But today. Today, my friend, we recognize you for who you truly are. The past is no more. Today is a new day!"

Ok, I'm taking license here, but I want to interject what a remarkable power we have when it comes to speaking life and positivity into the ears of our children, our students, and those we mentor. I always try to remember something when it comes to seeing my kids first thing in the morning and going to greet them after school. This, by the way, is another gem of a lesson that I see my wife live out in front of me each day.

First, I want to give them my undivided attention. The practice of putting off whatever is holding your attention at the moment for the sake of your child who enters the room is a tough one. I put down my phone, I look away from anything I am reading, and I go to make direct eye contact with them. I say, "Good morning, girl, I'm happy to see you" or "Hey Buddy, how were classes today?" Do I feel pressure to be fake, be a cheerleader, or generate an energy that is artificial and outside my personality? No. What I remember in those moments is that I am genuinely happy to see them, and I want them to know in that moment, they are all I am concerned with. Just like all moments with our kids, they are numbered, and that number is dropping daily.

These are MY kids and I love them dearly. When I look at them, I see my beautiful wife's face because she has made it her life's work to lead and love each one of them well. I also remember how blessed I am to have been called to partner with her and lead this family.

I can only imagine that when David saw Mephibosheth hobble into the room, he didn't see damaged goods. He saw a man of worth, just like when Jonathan first saw David fresh from the battlefield. Perhaps he saw the face of his dear brother Jonathan. Maybe his eyes began to well up with tears of joy as he remembered the promise he made to provide for his family. Scripture doesn't paint the literal picture for us to know what exactly happened after David enthusiastically yelled, "Mephibosheth!" Maybe he jumped off his throne and tackled the young man. Maybe he cupped the face of his brother's son in his hands and just gazed in silence while the court looked on awkwardly.

Mephibosheth's first act toward the king was to bow in honor and the next thing out of David's mouth would be much like Aragorn's response to the Hobbit's bowing down during the final moments of Peter Jackson's *The Lord of The Rings: Return of the King* film when the king thoughtfully rebukes, "you bow to no one." The King of Israel tells the shell-shocked Mephibosheth exactly what he is going to do next!

> *"I will surely show you kindness for the sake of your father Jonathan. I will restore to you all the land that belonged to your grandfather Saul, and you will always eat at my table."* 2 *Sam 9:7*

Did you get that? David just spoke the IPC into Mephibosheth!

Do you know who you are? You are the son of Jonathan! You are the grandson of Saul! You are royalty! (IDENTITY) and because of who you are, I am going to give back the land that is rightfully yours for you to manage it (PURPOSE), oh, and clear your schedule because from now on, you have a permanent place at my family table (COMMUNITY).

Mephibosheth's response? "Um, I think you got the wrong guy. I don't deserve this. I am a dog. And not even a cool dog like one of those YouTube bulldogs that wear sunglasses and ride a skateboard. I'm as useful and as valuable as a dead dog."

And David just keeps going like Willy Wonka when he rushes Charlie and Grandpa Joe into the glass elevator telling Charlie that he not only wins the chocolate, but he gets the whole factory too! So shines a good deed in a weary world, indeed.

David calls for Ziba and tells him that he and all his household will now serve Mephibosheth as they once served King Saul. He is giving Mephibosheth ALL the land that Saul was once responsible for and he tells Ziba and everyone else in ear shot once more that Mephibosheth will eat at the king's table every day.

The next verse tells us Mephibosheth ate at David's table with him and his family.

Every.

Day.

The final two verses of this marvelous chapter tell us three important things. First, Mephibosheth must have started doing something right on the social tip because before we know it, he has a son named Mika. Glad that worked out for Mephibosheth. The second thing we read is that Mephibosheth got to change his address and began getting all his mail forwarded to Jerusalem. So that's great because instead of being completely marginalized from culture as he was for years in Lo Debar, he could now enjoy life a little. Finally, we are reminded just once more that "he always ate at the king's table."

Why is it so important that within this short chapter of only 13 verses we, the readers, are told no fewer than four times that Mephibosheth got to eat with David and his family every day? I believe that COMMUNITY was the essential and difficult reality that David could instill into Mephibosheth's life (spoiler alert, I also think it's the most difficult component of life we can hope to experience or model for our kids as well).

Just as it was crazy that the accomplished David would sit on his throne wondering if there was anyone else to show kindness to, the fact he invited Mephibosheth to have a permanent seat at his table cannot be overlooked. Notice that David did not invite Mephibosheth over to Thanksgiving or Christmas dinner. This was not an invitation from an attitude of pity or patronizing self-indulgence. David could have very easily taken the photo opportunity with Mephibosheth and would have been seen as gracious and above board by simply recognizing his friend's son, giving him a portion of his land, and that could have been that.

But David didn't just give out of what trivial reserves he had to spare and would not miss. He gave to the point of inconvenience.

Other than a low opinion of himself that gets shared in one of the few times he is quoted in Scripture, we do not have a clear indication of Mephibosheth's personality. Maybe he was hilarious and kept everybody in stitches at the comedy club's open mic night in Lo Debar. However, it would not be a stretch to believe that Mephibosheth might have been...a bummer. He spent most of his life without purpose and with no real sense of identity borrowing a room from someone in a sleepy little town. He might have been a real Debbie Downer in situations. He probably kept to himself or could have been passive aggressive. Before he got a chance to know even a little bit about Jonathan's son, David committed himself (and his family) to daily meals with Mephibosheth passing the potatoes. Gordon Lightfoot's lyrics come to mind as he sings, "Sit down, young stranger, and tell us who you are."

This fact reveals a lot about David's identity and his commitment to prioritizing Mephibosheth's.

So maybe you've read a page or two of the Bible and you know more of King David's story. The next chapter after the account of David and Mephibosheth deals with David's victory in battle over the Ammonites and then one chapter later we read about a scandal that, if it took place today, it would most definitely turn into a major cover up. The short of it is King David covered up his act of adultery and theft by having a good and faithful soldier murdered. We are told David was successful in the covering up his sin but that the act displeased God. David and Bathsheba paid the price as the Lord took the life of their son. David mourned and then we are told upon hearing of his son's death, he went to the house of the Lord and worshipped him. The Lord then blessed David and Bathsheba with Solomon and the Bible tells us God loved Him and we read later Solomon was granted with ultimate wisdom and incomparable success.

So why is David such a great example for us as parents, teachers, and mentors to consider? Because like us, he was a walking and talking paradox. He was a lowly shepherd who lacked the credentials to become anything in this world, yet God called him as a nobody from nowhere to become King.

While most think that his sin over Bathsheba was the lowest of lows for him, we must remember the time he asked for an inventory of his fighting men in 2 Samuel 24 and the Bible says he was "conscience-stricken" after this and realized he had sinned against God. The amazing thing was that David never forgot what it was like to be in that position so when it came to blessing Mephibosheth by speaking Identity, Purpose, and Community into his heart, he was perfectly willing and able to do so.

The IPC Explained

There are countless things parents can pray over their children. That they respond to God's love for them by following Jesus. That they would be safe from harm. That they would be victorious in their sports. That they would have friends. That they would get into a particular college, training, or vocation. That they would always see themselves as valuable and loved.

These are all important and generally accepted across the board. These are great things to pray for as they each speak into two truths: 1) We as parents are powerless in many areas of our kids' lives and 2) We NEED God to work actively to provide from His goodness for our kids. Take a second and let these two truths sink in. It may be a hard pill to swallow for parents reading this who see themselves as the problem-fixer and ultimate authority in their household.

There are zero guarantees in parenting and investing in others. We have to TRUST in the fact we do not have all the answers or all the solutions to our kids' problems. We then get to pair that with the TRUTH that God does.

So, what happens when we begin to think about God actively shaping someone's identity, purpose, and community? Let's begin by taking a closer look at these parts of our kids' lives.

The backbone of this book lies in the understanding and application of some key terms that sum up the existence of those we invest in. This model gives parents, teachers, and mentors handlebars as to how we can pray over our people from before they are ever born to when they are adults living on their own. The "IPC" that will be covered throughout this book stands for IDENTITY, PURPOSE, and COMMUNITY. These three areas of a person's life are the most important aspects to consider and relate to each other in a way that will promote a holistic perspective when praying for and investing in a loved one.

We will discover how your identity is the core of who you are and that out of identity comes purpose: what a person does because of who they are. Because no one in history was ever created to live out his or her purpose in a vacuum isolated from people, we will consider how purpose is fully realized within the context of true community.

A person's optimal IDENTITY is discovered when they realize they are children of God, having been made in His image. Based on this fact, the created is free to discover their PURPOSE in life that is centered on obedience to whatever God is instructing them to do daily. IDENTITY and PURPOSE find their fulfillment within the context of COMMUNITY. One's community includes the nuclear and extended family, teams, friends, schoolmates, coworkers, church family, and even strangers.

Metaphorical Reasons

Another church parking lot I sat in one evening was a Methodist church in Houston where my family and friends met to watch a David Wilcox* concert in 2002. He was touring coffee shops and smaller venues at the time promoting his "Live Songs and Stories" album. On that record, he preempts a song with a short monologue called "Metaphorical Reasons" in which he describes touring the Biltmore House in Asheville, North Carolina. George Vanderbilt's sprawling mansion features 250 rooms, of which 35 are bedrooms and 43 bathrooms. It wasn't the ostentatious size of the home that bugged Wilcox but instead the fact Vanderbilt lived alone in his home. In essence, Wilcox couldn't reconcile how one person could live within so much emptiness. Maybe the best metaphor I can share when relating the IPC to you is that you would consider it as a home builder would.

A house's concrete foundation is an appropriate metaphor for identity. Jesus compares people who hear his words and do them to wise builders who build a home on a solid-rock foundation. These folks are safe when the storms of life hit because unlike the unwise who build on sandy soil (here today, gone tomorrow), a solid foundation can withstand disaster. So, a solid foundation never changes and serves as an excellent metaphor for the noun of our identity, aka who we are.

Purpose, or the action of what we do, can be understood as the dwelling structure of our lives that is quite literally built on the foundational identity of who we are. Just as a home builder spends time framing walls, adding a roof, wiring, plumbing, and installing details like trim and accessories, so purpose is a vast, thoughtful, and unending process.

Once identity and purpose are realized, just like a home, we have a structure that is ready to have others invited into it. Identity is the being, purpose is the doing, and community is inviting outsiders in. Just as Wilcox was annoyed for "metaphorical reasons" that the old mansion he toured belonged to a bachelor who never lit the darkness of all the home's 65 fireplaces, so the structure/purpose of our life only meets its potential when all the rooms of our hearts are full to capacity with love and service to people who are welcome to come in, pull up a comfortable chair, and warm themselves by the fire.

*Many thanks to my friend, Jim Walker, for introducing me to David Wilcox through his excellent album, *Home Again*, in college. To this day, I scarce can listen to "Let Them In" without getting a lump in my throat.

CHAPTER 2

A HEART NEEDS A HOME

(Identity is Essential)

I came to you when no one could hear me
I'm sick and weary of being alone
Empty streets and hungry faces
The world's no place when you're on your own
A heart needs a home
-from Richard Thompson's "A Heart Needs a Home"

My first interaction with a house's foundation was terrifying. A neighbor's golden retriever crawled under their house to have her puppies. That house on River Drive was built on a pier and beam foundation as opposed to a concrete slab. A pier and beam is unique in that vertical concrete or wooden piers resting on footers are strategically placed to support horizontal beams along the perimeter and under a house's subfloors. So, instead of a solid concrete foundation, many pier and beam houses have lots of space between the subfloor and ground.

My dad called my eight-year-old self over and we knelt in front of a small open panel and gazed into the black void as cool, moldy air breathed lightly into our faces. Though we could hear faint whimpers of fresh puppies somewhere in the still abyss, the only thing his flashlight revealed to us was the dusty reflection of spiderwebs hanging loosely in each corner from beam to pier and pier to ground. They gently swayed back and forth as if to say, "come in...come in...there's nothing here...to...harm you."

"That's a pretty tight fit me for, John David. Can you take this flashlight and try to get the dog to come out with her puppies?"

It was tough letting the man down in that moment, but I remember having my mind flooded with about fifty graphic images of how I would surely die under that house.

"Umm. No."

Years later, Mandi and I bought our own pier and beam farmhouse in Brenham, Texas, just across the street from Fireman's Park and the high school's baseball field. The five years we lived in the home were full of lively adventures that included waking up to a downpour resulting in rain drops on the dining room table and stuffing blankets in wavy-glass windowpanes and door thresholds while a freezing northerner blew through.

That old house was a classroom for me in construction and remodeling. We added a bathroom, enclosed a back porch, and even built a door jamb where a wall had been. (I loved it when my dad would come over and stand looking at the door and say, "I'm just so impressed you did that," while rubbing his chin.)

Something I say about wood is that it never forgets that it was once a tree. Many things made of wood have a way of moving and flexing over time. I've seen it for years with things like old houses and old skateboards.

Houses like our 1930-built pier and beam on Jeffries St were built so they could flex and breathe. It's why beadboard and shiplap are such good materials for old houses versus paneling and sheetrock. Every year our house on Jeffries would move slightly and we always noticed it when the front door would start sticking on the threshold. During the rainy, warmth of spring, the ground along the perimeter walls would expand slightly and the outer walls would rise while in the cold, dry season, the walls would drop back down. So, about twice a year it was my job to grab a flashlight, remove a panel on the house's skirting in the backyard and crawl on my belly for forty or fifty feet near the front door and either raise or lower the beam which ran under the center wall of our house so we could open, close, and lock our front door for the next four to six months.

Foundations are important. Strong foundations are the difference between weathering the storms of life or being utterly devastated and destroyed. The best foundations, whether pier and beam or concrete slab, are those that are rooted beyond the shifting sand and soils of what we can see and into secure and stable bedrock. Jesus spoke of building components in comparing the wise and the foolish within his famous Sermon on the Mount (Matt 5-7).

Several years after Jesus spoke these words, the Apostle Paul picked up the metaphor in a letter he wrote to the young church in Ephesus that needed to learn the lesson of unity and acceptance as they were learning there was no longer a need to stress the differences between Jews and Gentiles:

"You are no longer foreigners and strangers, but fellow citizens with God's people and also members of his household, *built on the foundation* of the apostles and prophets, with *Christ Jesus himself as the chief cornerstone.* In him the whole building is joined together and rises to become a holy temple in the Lord. And in him *you too are being built together to become a dwelling in which God lives by his Spirit.*" Eph 2:19-22

Identity Everywhere

There is no telling how many times I let the cursor blink as my frozen fingers hovered over the keyboard on this section. While there has never been more fodder to examine in recent years than on the topic of identity, I am as overwhelmed by the issue as I am exhausted by the circular reasoning, petty arguments, and soul-crushing sadness that so many people are going through worldwide as they wrestle with themselves and each other over the answers to who am I and how can I feel like I matter?

While having a clear understanding of one's own identity is critical to one's mental health and quality of life, the issue is far greater that. Identity crisis is a daily issue for many. The very definition of what it even means to be human will be even harder to understand and explain as technology and virtual reality expand by leaps and bounds.

To understand the unchanging definition of who you are is a wonderful thing. Having a clear idea of your identity is perhaps the most important thing you can have established if you are to be any good to anybody in life (starting with yourself). How can you know what you're supposed to do if you have no idea of who you are?

Ironically, this most important thing about us is so very hard for many people to realize. And why wouldn't it be if you have suffered abuse or neglect by the hands of those who should have been the ones helping you to figure out your unique identity that speaks into your uncompromising value? In my own life, I can remember an influential family member saying that I am nothing more than a "bottom feeder" with no hope of becoming much. The power of words spoken over us, even when we know in the moment they are false or come from a pain we can't be responsible for, still leave a mark.

What Identity Is Not: Profession or Purpose

Like most members of the ex-covid human race, I went to see Top Gun: Maverick in the theater. While I soaked up every scene and every line of the deliciously self-indulgent film, there was a line that bugged me. In the scene, Maverick is with Iceman. He is struggling to see his own worth and wrestling with matters of identity and purpose. He delivers the line, "being a jetfighter *is not what I do*, it is *who I am*." So, even the heroes of our imagination struggle to know the difference between identity and purpose.

Identity is not a profession. As a grown man, if I walk up to another grown man and ask him to tell me about himself, he will identify himself by his job title. It makes sense as it's the thing he spends the bulk of his waking hours doing and it's the way he provides for himself and his family. It's also the thing he worked hard to gain training or education in so, again, makes a lot more social sense to answer "I'm a tech at chemical manufacturing plant" than answering something more accurate to true identity.

Identity is not purpose. Identity is who you are. Purpose is what you do based on who you are. Writer and spiritual director, Richard Rohr, shares a helpful analogy for explaining this relationship by stating that all people need a place to stand and a lever to work. Realizing your identity is understanding you have been created and that you, as a human being, have a right to take up an average of 1.76 cubic feet of volume on planet earth. It's sad that we at times are filled with such insecurity in life that we feel we are in the wrong for occupying such a small area on the earth's surface. Rohr would say (based on the premise of Greek philosopher, Archimedes) that our identity is realized when we discover that there is indeed a place specifically allotted on this green and blue orb designed just for us. He might also say that our purpose is realized once we discover that we have a lever to work (or a way to make the world a better place by investing in someone). However, the danger is when we confuse our human doing for human being.

To Be a Seated Soul

One of the biggest leaps of faith I've ever taken in my life was when my family made the transition to Waco which included leaving two decades of church staff leadership and all the comforts that it included (I'm looking at you, medical insurance!).

Part of the transition included pursuing, then ultimately cancelling, the notion the unrest I was dealing with at the time would be alleviated by simply finding a new church to work at. A friend of mine who lived in west Houston reached out around this time and said that I should apply to work at her church as they were looking for a youth minister.

Days later, I was sitting across from her pastor at a Chinese restaurant in Sealy, Texas. Somewhere between the egg drop soup and sesame chicken, he introduced me to the idea of being a "seated soul." It was a timely and profound metaphor for how to live a life as I was struggling with what I hope was my final identity crisis at the time (I know, never say never). As I sat listening to the middle-aged pastor talk about what it means to operate from a place of confident security and intention, I remember wondering if the mentoring moment I was having meant I needed to take the job and hear some wisdom from this guy on an almost daily basis or if I was to heed his words and take them with me as the Barnard family set sail for new horizons.

The offer looked great on paper, however the decision to start another tenure within conventional youth ministry leadership at a church was, thankfully, not meant to be. My new pastor friend did not take the news well. When I explained the premise of taking Middleman full-time, he said pointing ministry at a niche group like teenagers interested in skateboarding, art, and music would include never-ending fundraising and there wouldn't be enough folks who cared about that kind of kid to keep it going. He was right about the fundraising, but he couldn't have been more wrong about finding a critical mass of people who care about "that kind of kid."

His notion of the "seated soul" dovetailed well into Archimedes' "place to stand and lever to operate" theory. When you operate from a place of understanding your identity and purpose, you can focus on community building. A seated soul is of great use to young people aimlessly and anxiously looking for ways to define and justify their existence.

The Airplane Metaphor

I'm a car guy. I always have been. My grandmother had this colorful rug under her dining room table that was full of these amoeba-type shapes that formed a network of imagined "roadways" throughout the rug that I'd spend hours driving my Hot Wheels over. One of my favorite vehicles was an 18-wheeler rig that had a little steering wheel at the back of the trailer you could use to steer the cab. That truck had me working long shifts on that rug as "BJ and the Bear" and Snowman from "Smokey and the Bandit." Even today, I try to convince Mandi that we need to see the country as a long-distance trucking team, pulling long hauls while listening to Red Simpson songs on the radio and eating at greasy spoons across the U.S. (She's not convinced. Yet.)

As parents, we've never wanted the lack of wealth to keep us from prioritizing travel as a family. Since our kids were little, we made it a point to take road trips. Over the years, our family has logged tens of thousands of miles and has driven all over Texas, to the west coast from Washington to So Cal and in the east from Pennsylvania to the Florida Keys. Mandi's a wizard at finding affordable hotels and camp sites and we're no happier than when we're wandering through the trees in state parks or taking in the sites downtown Anywhere, USA.

We do this for two reasons: one, we really like our kids and we have always wanted to spend as much time with them as possible because we believed it when we were told that with kids the days are long, but the years are short. The second reason for our prioritizing our road trips is we always wanted our kids to know there's a bigger world out there than the local community we raised them in. Living in smalltown Texas for most of our kids' formative years showed us something. For all their chicken-fried charm, small towns can indirectly convince kids that what's going on there is all they need to be concerned with.

Visiting as many states as we have over the years exposed

us to different cultures and gave our kids an appreciation for how other people live. This can be a valuable lesson for our kids and can give parents tons of teachable moments as they see God's handiwork in the awe-inspiring expanse of the Grand Canyon, the wonder of watching a dolphin swim within a wave while being silhouetted against the setting sun behind the Pacific Ocean (yeah, this actually happened one day in San Diego), or how kindness and connection are still on display between people who don't share a common language on the streets of Chinatown.

As much as I love family road trips, I hate flying. I have anxiety the night before travelling by plane because of all the hurry up and wait involved. The drive to the airport. The finding a parking spot. The taking a shuttle bus. The standing in line for checking in luggage praying with all your might it's under 50lbs. The standing in line to take off your shoes and belt. The holding your arms up while getting ogled by the cameras. The chance you could get patted down if the cameras don't like what they see. The waiting for your flight. The standing in line to get on the plane and on and on it goes.

But one part of flying relates well to the concept of identity and gives parents, teachers, and mentors something to remember. It's the part about how, in the event of an emergency, masks will drop down from the ceiling which should help keep you alive if you're not already good and dead from hitting a mountainside. The flight attendant is always good about reminding parents and adults to put on their own mask before helping their younger traveling companion with theirs. This instruction is given because it's human nature to be so concerned with the objects of our affection and protection we may forget to see to ourselves first. The problem with addressing our kids' needs without addressing our own is that to help them, we must first make sure we're good to go or else we're both in trouble.

The account of David and Mephibosheth would have looked a lot different if David hadn't been in a healthy place with his identity, purpose, and community. Had David been feeling insecure or unsure of himself he wouldn't have been as generous. Had he needed something from Mephibosheth, his love would have been conditional.

In relating to our kids, students, and mentees we need to have already had our IPC firmly established. We need to come to them from a place of margin so we can be about them and not ourselves. While it's never necessary to pretend you have all the answers in life, being comfortable in your own skin, working to be a seated soul, and having a strong sense of your identity will be its own encouragement for those you invest in as you set the tone for a healthy relationship.

Pitfalls to Avoid When Parenting/Mentoring

It's dangerous and irresponsible, yet often tempting, to solicit our identity from children or mentees. This can happen without us even knowing. Spending decades in youth ministry and church leadership gave me the opportunity to see how a lot of people parented before we had kids ourselves. I'm sure everybody wants to be the "cool parents" who have the pool in the backyard or the game room upstairs where all the teenage friends are welcome to hang out anytime. But there were a few occasions when some parents took their involvement a step too far and lost sight of the much-needed line between adult and teen.

Living Vicariously Through our Teenagers

The sin analogy of the frog slowly boiling in the pot relates well to this parenting pitfall. After all, the intent is pure. We all want to stay engaged with our teenagers as they navigate relationships and turning the corner from truly leading our kids to shifting to a more supportive role can be a hard pill to swallow. But as so many parents fight to stay active in their kids' social lives, there is a point where a line needs to be drawn.

I got a call one afternoon from a mom in our church who asked if I could come over and talk to her daughter whose dating relationship with a boy had ended. Both teenagers were active in our youth group, and they made a popular couple. Their parents also hit it off well and it was common for the families to spend ample amounts of time together. They were so connected they'd take vacations together and even spend every Sunday evening after church alternating between each of their houses.

When I arrived at the girl's house I can remember being taken aback when the mother of the teenager opened the door in tears and quickly went in for a hug as I stood on the front step with my mind racing as to what kind of disaster had taken place. Was there a death in the family? Had her daughter been so out of sorts with this break up that she did something drastic?

Once we made it to the living room and the mother prompted her daughter to tell me what had happened, it proved to be far less traumatic. The two high school students' dating relationship had run its course, so they decided to break up. That's it. Everyone was still alive, and no property had been damaged due the breakup. The real casualty from this relationship that was no more was in the mom's heart. To stay connected with her daughter, she put herself too close to the teenage relationship. She was invested. She had hopes and dreams for what it would mean when those two kids would go off to college together, get married soon after, move into a house down the street from her, and shower her with all the grandbabies.

While talking to the mom, it was clear that the boy hadn't just broken up with her daughter, he had broken up with the mom as well. And that's where the problem lies. It's great for parents and mentors to stay connected with their kids and mentees, knowing their struggles, and feeling empathy for their pain but it shouldn't be at the cost of their uncompromised identity and purpose. Yes, we want to relate well to our kids, but the title of "parent" or "mentor" should always outrank that of "friend."

A Heavy Load to Bear

Getting too close to the relationships our kids are discovering is just one of the pitfalls we should avoid while leading teenagers well. Another is that of expectation. This makes sense as like everything else, we expect a return on investment (ROI) of our money and our time. Say you spend years meeting with your mentee throughout his junior high and high school years. Maybe you spend thousands of dollars helping with his physical needs. This can lead us to feel we have earned the right to direct his path and determine his destiny; after all we want what is best for him. But this too can be dangerous as the mentor is often just one voice (if not the only voice) speaking health and consistency into the heart of a mentee. You can spend countless hours and dollars on a mentee and still have her disappoint you with her life choices that don't live up to your expectations.

Don't Give to Get

We all love the story of the influential teacher/coach who takes a rag tag bunch of students or athletes and turns them into winners. We've seen it in films like *Lean on Me, Stand and Deliver, Remember the Titans*, etc. The problem with this motivation for investing in others is it can often turn conditional or sour when we don't get the Disney ending that we feel we deserve. The mentor who needs affirmation or recognition from her mentee may ultimately cut off the mentoring relationship if the mentee doesn't reciprocate the support. In this age of social media, there is also the danger of making sure that your selfless act of investment gets documented well and shared with many so others will see just how active you are within your mentoring program. The true fallout here is when a mentee feels less like the object of a mentor's affection and more like the mechanism used to advertise the mentor's brand to her virtual community.

As a mentor or as a parent, how can you introspectively assess whether your identity is solid before working to help your mentee or child discover there's?

This question is answered by understanding the source of where we find things. Early in my dating relationship with Mandi it became clear that I depended on her heavily for my spiritual development. How did this tendency rear its ugly head? First and foremost, it was clear if Mandi was at church on a Sunday morning so was I. But on days when she wasn't going to be there, I was open to taking the morning off by sleeping in or finding something else to do. That tendency revealed she was the determining factor on whether I went to church. It's common for us as men to prioritize our faith based on what a woman in our life is going to think about it.

Although I love Mandi more than any other person on earth, she is not my Savior. While she's a virtuous woman, she doesn't possess the ability to redeem my soul or even validate my existence. That's a job only God can do. When David identified Mephibosheth as Jonathan's son and gave him purpose in leadership, he was not lacking in either of these areas himself. David was a man after God's heart, and his benevolence to Mephibosheth was not how the title was to be attained, but instead a natural outpouring of it.

CHAPTER 3

THE PRETENDER

(Identity is Forever)

Caught between the longing for love
And the struggle for the legal tender
Where the sirens sing and the church bells ring
And the junk man pounds his fender
Where the veterans dream of the fight
Fast asleep at the traffic light
And the children solemnly wait
For the ice cream vendor
Out into the cool of the evening
Strolls the pretender
He knows that all his hopes and dreams
Begin and end there
-from Jackson Browne's "The Pretender"

South Houston, Tx sits next to Pasadena, just east of I-45. Its perfectly rectangular shape is crossed diagonally by Highway 3 to Galveston and horizontally by College/Spencer Highway. The town, originally named Dumont, was founded by C. S. Woods of the Western Land Company in 1907. A post office was established three years later, and by 1913, Dumont was incorporated as South Houston. During those early years, commerce grew as local growers shipped local produce, including strawberries, figs, and vegetables, along the Galveston, Houston, and Henderson Railroads. Many businesses that emerged by that time were destroyed by a 1915 hurricane. The newly constructed Houston Ship Channel helped the development of heavy industries further inland. The city's potential grew through the manufacturing of railroad equipment, toys, masonry, candy, and even an early airplane.

The small town grew rapidly during the 1940s to the early 1960s. George Christy served as the city's mayor from 1949 to 1951 and then again in 1960 to 1964. Since Christy owned a circus, the colorful businessman employed the use of his performing elephants to help build Spencer Highway. In the sixties, South Houston's population was just over 7,000 and the city had attracted numerous industries and manufacturers of asphalt, concrete conduits, wire products, and oilfield chemicals. Within twenty years, the population would nearly double, but commerce shifted to mostly retail and service industries. Today, South Houston is a community of over 16,000 residents. More than ninety percent of its citizens are Hispanic, and the average household income is just above $45,000 (2020).

Like many folks, I am proud of where I come from. Some of my first substantial memories of growing up in South Houston include riding my bike to Fernandez Meat Market for barbacoa and sweet bread to eat while watching local wrestling early on TV Saturday mornings. By the time I was in high school, I had covered every street within the square three-miles of South Houston on foot, bike, skateboard, or behind the wheel of my 1976 Buick LeSabre four-door gifted to me by my Uncle David in 1991. Unlike today, when we know exactly where our kids are because we have an app that tracks their every move, growing up in the 80s in South Houston meant our parents only knew we were going "out" and that we'd be back home "later." Yes, it was sketchy, but how else were fellow fourth-grader Jeff Nichols and I supposed to be free to shoplift from K-Mart or throw rocks at the back wall of the Double J Icehouse from behind the dumpster of the empty lot next door?

Many of the residential blocks in South Houston are laid out in a grid pattern with alphabet lettered avenues running east to west and numbered streets running north and south. Many of my formative years were spent traveling those streets and, because of a daily commitment to skateboarding between the ages of 11 to 18, skating in those parking lots with their jungle gyms of parking blocks, poured concrete inclines, and metal rails.

The house on Avenue F is where I grew up through much of elementary school. I would spend as much time as possible at the public pool and softball fields that were just a few blocks down the street. It was on one fateful summer day as I schlepped down the street as a common pedestrian after swimming at the pool that I discovered it.

Jutting from an ample pile of furniture and clothes on the patch of grass between the street and the empty house's front ditch was what appeared to be a blue plastic skateboard with yellow wheels. I stood questioning the reliability of my nine-year-old eyes. It was common to see a large pile of a house's contents next to the street in South Houston. Many houses were rental properties and when folks moved out, or were evicted, their personal belongings and furniture were usually thrown out on the yard on the edge of the street for city workers to come collect. But to have my eyes averted to something of such great value like what I saw that day was certainly an anomaly.

Like an emboldened adventurer determined to conquer K2, I remember setting my threadbare towel and flattened Capri Sun pouch on a patch of grass as far away from the late-July ant beds as I could, and quickly began making my way up the jagged and treacherous mound of broken dreams, eyes fixed on its shining monument of endless possibilities pointing in plastic perfection heavenward. Once standing atop trash mountain, I grasped the warm alloy metal truck of the board with both hands like a young Arthur hoping to loosen Excalibur from the discerning stone. One slippery flip flop fought for traction on a brown veneer dresser, the other slowly sank within a bunched-up and stained window curtain resting on Good Housekeeping magazines and newspapers. I strained upward with eyes closed tight and teeth clenched to shield the white-hot and unbridled power the soon-to-be rescued freedom machine would surely emit like a large rippling circle of glory akin to an earth strike by Thor's Mjölnir.

In the next instant, angels' sweet melodies and hazy clouds of grandeur subsided. I opened my eyes and focused on the treasure within my grasp. I silently mouthed the words molded onto the plastic deck's top: "GT...Coyote... II...Grentec...California." As the board was buried nose-first in the pile, I quickly discovered what many would consider a tragedy in the form of a naked, threaded axle tip exposed with nary a self-locking nut, bearing, washer, or yellow urethane wheel in sight.

Had it not been for destiny's reassuring hand upon my shoulder and wind beneath my wings that day, I could have reset the unearthed object of rejection back atop its funeral pyre, scaled down the cigarette-fragranced mountain with empty hands, and continued the short walk home with only hopes of Monterrey House cheese enchiladas and the evening's broadcast of the A-Team to brighten my countenance. But instead, I basked in the excitement of my discovery.

I immediately set the board down on its three existing wheels, and slowly pushed myself home down Avenue F having no idea that the GT Coyote's squeaky bearings and South Houston's less than optimal concrete would harmonize to create music to my ears with a song I still enjoy hearing today. (Non-skater note: It's unfashionable in skateboarding to push your skateboard with your front foot. To push "mongo" is frowned upon by those who feel it doesn't look cool enough. The irony of not doing something a certain way because it's deemed "unpopular" in skateboarding is noteworthy. I grew up pushing my skateboard the "wrong" way because my first skateboard was missing a front wheel, so I had to concentrate my weight with my back foot over the rear truck on the board to keep the front axle from digging into the concrete and sending me over the top of it into another dimension. While I later taught myself how to push effectively using either foot, I will occasionally push mongo to remember the pure joy that skateboarding gave to me that day as a nine-year-old.)

I grew up mostly living with my family comprised of my stepfather, Armando, my mom, my older sister Sara, and younger siblings Anna, Adam, Amber, and Alicia in South Houston. I also spent a short time living in a nearby part of Houston with my dad, stepmom, Janis, and siblings, Johanna and Andy. For those keeping track, I am one of eight children divided between two homes – one was the Guevara's and the other the Barnard's. The years I spent living with the Guevaras included visiting my dad's/the Barnards with my sister Sara every other weekend.

Like many families, there was a level of emotional pain in each home which led to poor choices, separation, and regret. At the end of the day, I believe both sets of parents did the best they could with the tools they were given at the time. Without a hint of blame or insult against any of my parents, I struggled at times in my upbringing to feel completely rooted as a complete family member. I attribute it to spending most of my life before adulthood with Guevaras while being a Barnard but also living with Barnards for two weekends a month out of a suitcase. There always seemed to be something in the way of my being entirely at home.

Identity Discovered: 100% Skateboarder

I don't know what became of my three-wheeled plastic skateboard. It was replaced one early Christmas morning when I came out to the tree and my mom pulled from beneath it a radiantly neon Sure Grip International with yellow and black checkered wheels and a light blue and yellow spiral graphic with the word "ZONER" screened across the middle of the board. I promptly jumped on the board, skated halfway down the sidewalk, and fell off. This was the first time in my life to ride a brand-new skateboard and the perfect wheels and new bearings offered more quiet speed than I could handle for even a twelve-foot ride.

If my trash pile Coyote board had hooked me on the feeling of skateboarding, it was on my Christmas Sure Grip that endeared the culture and started me on the path to realize my identity, purpose, and community as a 100% skateboarder.

From that point on, I had no other use for anything in life that did not have to deal with skateboarding. Without knowing it, I was working to shape my identity as a skateboarder. This is the title I would hope anyone who looked at me would use from now on. I dressed like a skater, talked like a skater, walked like a skater, and thought like a skater. With this identity came a sharpening of my purpose: to spend as much of my life as I could on a skateboard. All I needed to do to make the parents happy was to keep the solid Bs coming in school. I could do that without ever actually doing homework at home. I just did it in homeroom and during lunch every day.

Having skated for nearly forty years now, I meet many people my age who will tell me they used to skate. I always like to ask why they stopped, and the answer is usually, "my friends stopped skating, I started playing sports, I got my license and then a job..." It is usually a friend that gets somebody into skating and it's interesting that a lack of community will typically be a reason why they stopped. My community as a junior high skater was set in friendships with guys like Charlie Cjuko, John Rainwater, and his brother Jimmy as the core. I credit Charlie for his kindness in giving me my first "pro model" skateboard in the shape of a Lester Kasai Oak Leaf Tracker model that hangs today on my shop wall next to my desk. The nose and tail of the Lester are distant memories and the beat-up deck hangs as a reminder of a time when we had no choice but to ride a board until it was unrideable. (He was a meathead, but after a kid named Johnny snapped his Santa Cruz Rob Roskopp while we were street skating one day, he came back an hour later with a flat ¾" thick piece of pine with his trucks attached he cut with a jig saw using the broken deck as a template for the shape. We probably smirked and called him a kook at the time [under our breath of course because Johnny was bigger than us] but what he did that day was about the most punk rock and core skater thing you could do.)

My skateboarding community grew when I moved across the street from Zeek Garcia in eighth grade. He and I hung out daily for the next five years and Zeek remains as one of my best friends today. Our default spot was the Food City parking lot at the end of our block. Soon after moving to the house on Washington, I met Jesse Caltzonzint who, at that point, was the best skateboarder I had ever spent time with. Skating with Jesse was beneficial as he was my first friend who could ollie high enough to do handrails. My skating developed quickly because of Jesse's skill and example.

When a milestone in sports is finally reached, you may notice that other athletes quickly begin to accomplish the same feat. This happens with runners' times and with certain tricks in skating. I was watching skaters attempt to jump a gap in a pool competition and it was clear that no one would be successful. A small group of professionals tried over and over, and no one could land it. Until someone did. And then, the next skater landed it, followed by yet another. It was as if everyone was being conditioned to believe the gap was too immense right up until the time the first skater landed it. Once that happened, a switch went off in everyone's brain which said that the trick was, indeed, possible.

So whether it's skateboarding, learning how to play a musical instrument, discovering a new STEM concept, or adding another skill to our parenting toolbox, it is vital we put ourselves in contact with those who are "better" than us so we can have the switch in our brains go from "impossible" to "attainable."

The IPC model I was living through skateboarding was a good warm up for understanding the bigger picture of what these things could mean beyond the narrow and limited scope of skating. Once I saw there was a bigger world out there than *Thrasher Magazine* and the latest skate company's video, I discovered the difference between the temporal and eternal.

Forever or For Now

It is difficult to tell the difference between what is eternal and what is merely temporal. Some days seem to last forever. Some people never seem to change. Things get even tougher when we throw a good measure of fear and emotion into the equation. It's these two culprits that affect us like nothing else. How often do we make rash decisions based on a high degree of fear, our own emotions, or not taking time to gather more information? Some of the biggest mistakes of my life have been the ones I made without taking a beat and waiting for clear thought and perspective to influence my response to a situation.

What an incredibly practical tool Paul the Apostle used when writing to the Corinthians that one could "take captive every thought to make it obedient to Christ." No matter your faith tradition, we probably all learned about the direct connection between our thoughts, words, and actions while growing up. As the line goes, be careful of each of them because they become the next. Imagine living your life in such a way that even the smallest decisions would echo in some way for eternity. I don't think that's over-spiritualizing anything. As Paul was encouraging the young church, so I ask you to consider the notion that as thoughts get entertained in your mind, run each through a filter or lens to evaluate if it is life-giving or life-threatening. This is especially helpful for young men who seem to turn hurt and sadness so quickly into anger and aggression.

While in college, I drove by the full student parking lot of a local high school on a weekday. Police cars, ambulances, and fire engines were everywhere. An unthinkable thing had taken place just hours earlier that morning and the body of a young girl was found in her parked car. The story that was released just days later was heartbreaking. Apparently, the girl's boyfriend broke up with her and instead of seeking the help of a friend, teacher, or counselor, she walked out to her car and ended her life.

It's shocking to think that a thing like that could happen, but folks lacking support and perspective make decisions like this every day. All because the temporal and eternal can seem like the same thing in the heat of the moment. How significant would it have been to spend an hour listening to that young girl share her pain, ask her questions, feel her emptiness, and cry her tears? Imagine how vital it could have been to speak truth and value into her heart and give her a glimpse into how much circumstances would improve a year from now, a week from now, or by the next morning because she is not alone in her abandoned feelings and fears.

The work of the mentor and parent is often simply revealing that a future beyond the present struggle exists, and it is wonderful. This approach to living shows there is a hope to be had against perspectives like Jackson Browne's excellent "The Pretender." If you've never heard it, the song's mood and lyrics share the story of one experiencing a degree of lonely hopelessness when he laments over the repetition and soul-crushing disappointment found in the "struggle for the legal tender." May we, as people of highly defined identity, be a well spring of comfort to those needing to develop it in their lives.

The Forever of Identity
(Siempre Por Familia)

All people are first and foremost created. Biologically, two elements combined to create one. Pretty simple and no real need to argue that. To understand yourself and all people as created by the Creator is to realize all humans are made in the image of God. No matter what ways we invent to outrank each other, what titles we hold, or things that we accomplish to give us more (or less) value here in this life, this identity is never diminished and never becomes irrelevant. It is the very bedrock of who we are and that which our purpose is built upon. Our identity is eternal and therefore it is non-negotiable. Our identity as image-bearers of our Creator is enjoyed even before it is realized.

The Only Forever

One of the graphics we produce for Middleman is our "Siempre por Familia" slogan that we print on our boards and apply to our shirts. This truth is powerful and hits me on multiple levels. The translation of the Spanish is "Family Always." These words allow us to teach a basic theological truth to skaters and teenagers we meet through our skate ministry.

There always has been and there always will be just one thing: FAMILY (Dom Toretto agrees). Genesis 1 shares that before creation and on that side of eternity, the Spirit was hovering over the void. In John 1 it says that nothing was made without the Son making it so. The basis for our understanding the Trinity is simple: family existed for eternity through the Father, Son, and Holy Spirit before anything was ever created.

So why did the Godly "family" decide to create?

This heavenly party was much like when you're having a good time with friends and you think, "Man, I need to see what Stevie's doing, he'd love this!" The beauty of Creation is that once the Trinity started firing off materializing things by the utterance of a word, they (God) saw that it was good and wanted the party to grow. So, on the sixth day, Creation is perfected by the gathering of some soil and the breathing into it. Humanity is created as the only part of Creation which holds the unique title of image-bearer. Everything else on earth and in the cosmos is indeed impressive yet nothing compares to the design and potential of the human being. No other organism on earth can relate to God quite like people do.

Ironically, human beings work tirelessly to downplay their importance on this planet (see the advancements of AI, modern pet products and services that treat animals better than some humans, and the travesty of "speciesism"). For many, this priority stems from abuse of some kind or lack of an influence in their lives which allowed for healthy identity discovery.

How does it make you feel to understand that you, my friend, are God's finest handiwork? What would it take for you to see folks in your life, on social media, and even on the news as creations intended to live as eternal members of God's family?

> *"The Spirit you received does not make you slaves, so that you live in fear again; rather, the Spirit you received brought about your adoption to sonship. And by him we cry, 'Abba, Father.' The Spirit himself testifies with our spirit that we are God's children. Now if we are children, then we are heirs—heirs of God and co-heirs with Christ, if indeed we share in his sufferings in order that we may also share in his glory." Romans 8:15-17*

CHAPTER 4

CAN'T TRUSS IT

(Identity Through Self-Denial)

I know where I'm from, not dum diddie dum
From the base motherland
The place of the drum
Invaded by the wack diddie wack
Fooled the black, left us faded
King and chief probably had a big beef
Because of dat now I grit my teeth
So here's a song to the strong
'Bout a shake of a snake
And the smile went along with that
Can't truss it
-from Public Enemy's "Can't Truss It"

Chuck D's words resonate with those of Jesus when he spoke to and taught about the brood of vipers and white-washed tombs in the Bible. He was talking about those men in power and influence at the time: political and religious leaders who hurled self-righteousness and judgment at the weak to control them in the name of God.

Power has always been the shortest route to corruption.

We are all, each one of us, guilty of the crime, no matter how big our sandbox. The propensity to mishandle and squander our position for fleeting moments of comfort should remind us often that we indeed, can't truss it.

How refreshing it is to look at several occurrences recorded in the Gospels where Jesus interacted with the "least of these" within his social hierarchy. Included is the woman at the well where he contrasts the temporal well water with the eternal Living Water he offers. Elsewhere we see the quiet courage of the bleeding woman who knew that the frayed edge of Jesus' garment held enough power in it to give her relief. And another time still, while Jesus is leading a Bible study with his closest friends, a mother from a foreign land comes adamantly into the room begging for the Son of David to heal her demon-possessed daughter. The disciples' knee jerk response remains consistent (see feeding the 5,000) – "send her away!" What comes next is my favorite – Jesus with the zinger, "The bread that is meant for the children shouldn't go to the dogs." Whoa! Let that one marinate on your brain for a beat. Did Jesus just call the Canaanite woman a dog? Is this racism? Sexism?

Be careful here, because as soon as you start feeling the urge to fear that your felt-board Jesus prejudices and projections are in question, just know that it was the intent of this passage to make you feel discomfort and unrest because, sorry, but without getting stirred up, you will probably miss the point.

As this is indeed spiritual batting practice for his guys (and us as modern readers of Scripture) Jesus lobs the pitch right down the middle offering the desperate mom the ultimate home run as she then says:

> *"Even the dogs eat the crumbs that fall from their master's table." Matthew 15:27*

Boom. Woman, he says, you get it. And in that moment her daughter is whole again.

Were the women whose voices and actions recorded in the Bible any better than the men who seemed to struggle so much learning even simple lessons (looking at you, Peter, after Jesus got shiny on the mountain)? We could spend volumes talking about women like Miriam, Deborah, Esther, and Lydia from the Old Testament. For our purposes, let's not focus on "value" but instead primed potential.

Women in scripture had a shorter path to realizing the power of Jesus was limitless because they had been thoroughly stripped of their own. This is vital for us to realize as we consider Jesus' paradoxical teachings.

We Love Jesus, Yes We Do, We Love Jesus, How Bout YOU?!?!

I spend a fair amount of my life standing in line at big box hardware stores. On one such occasion, a conversation between two grown men started up nearby and sounded something like, "Y'all took care of business yesterday!!!" "Yeah, I wasn't expecting (someone's last name) to even play after being out for the month!" "Good luck against 'Bama" "Hell yeah, we'll need it. Don't y'all get a bye this week?" "Yeah, but then USC (inflated cheeks, slow release of breath out clinched lips)" and then the conversation initiator headed out the door while pulling sunglasses from the back of his neck to the bridge of his nose.

That exchange is one reason I don't take out and stare at my phone while in line. I would have otherwise missed out on enjoying the fascinating interaction of humanity. I liked how the one guy who initiated the dialogue never stopped sliding his Hey Dudes across the concrete floor as he exited the store. He barely even made eye contact. He just didn't have to.

To make sense of the exchange, you must know that one of the men was wearing a t-shirt and coordinating cap with a university's name and mascot on them while the other man was wearing another university's logo on a visor that had fake spiky and multi-colored hair haloed by the visor's fabric headband (just imagine him looking like Guy Fiera, because he did).

I love that sport is a unifier for many. Families maintain generational pride in supporting college and professional athletic programs and for many men throughout history, connecting with their children and other men is best done within the parameters of sports involvement and enjoyment.

Want to see me cry dehydrating tears? Pop in (yes in a VCR) *Field of Dreams* and watch me get hit with all the emotions but especially a guaranteed stream down my cheeks at "Hey Dad...wanna have a catch?" at the end. Forget about it. I'm physically tired after that movie.

Sports also offers us a duality in our thinking that can sometimes mar our spirituality. Often, if I am for one team it means I am directly opposed to another. I can remember attending a youth camp in the late 80s with campers sitting in bleachers on both sides of a gym. To get all the kids really excited about whatever they needed to be excited about, a "We love Jesus..." cheer was started by the rec team and ample time was spent with both mobs of teenagers yelling the statement followed by the question at each other and each time it was yelled the volume and aggressive energy increased. It was competitive. It was silly. It was weird. But it was the 80s.

Jesus understood our need for and struggle with duality and dichotomous reasoning. He leaned in on the matter during the Sermon on the Mount and other teachings throughout the Gospels as he presented a comparing and contrasting between what we think we know and what is reality.

"You've heard this preached at you, but I'm here to tell you something else. The first will be last. The leader will be a servant. The greatest will be the least. And, by the way, how you treated the least? That's what you also did to me."

It's as if, in our tireless search for significance (identity), we work to differentiate ourselves from others. To think ourselves better than. To earn. To win.

I'm afraid we're pointing our oversized foam finger in the wrong direction.

Jesus gently reminds us that our worship of God is most defined by how we serve, consider, and connect to those in Creation we have the most difficult time valuing.

Here's one practical way to start doing this better.

Healthy and Unhealthy vs Good and Bad

Words matter. Choosing them wisely is an art. We taught our kids early on that vulgar and coarse language aren't inherently evil and hold no power in themselves, but they do represent a thought process and subsequent heart condition.

The Head, Heart, Hands model of teaching is one I read about years ago. I don't know where it came from, but I use it every time I preach or teach to ensure the lesson finds a place to land. Briefly stated, it means that if I am communicating a truth to someone, I want to first make sure it makes sense to their brains by connecting at the head level. I believe truths that God reveals to us do not need to stop there. I want these principles to leak their way down into the listener's heart, or the place within him far beyond what he will merely nod his head in agreement with. Truths from God's word are what often get used to construct our ideology and worldview as we "take them to heart."

But a truth can only realize its potential in action.

So, if I stand before a congregation and connect a passage of scripture to their brains and see it through to fortify them on the heart level but I give them no ways to consider applying all the "amens" to life beyond the pew, it's as useful as placing your car up on blocks before taking it for a drive – wheels still spin, nobody gets anywhere. What we think (head), what we believe (heart), and what we do (hands) are supposed to be connected. So again, words matter.

Using your vocabulary to best communicate your thoughts and beliefs is a credit to yourself and a blessing to others. The only issue with vulgar or inappropriate language is that for every immoral/forbidden/unsavory adjective or noun you spew when feeling small, hurt, or angry, there are multiple more accurate and relevant words left dormant.

Christians' relationship with language is a funny one. This is best understood when considering the commandment to not take the Lord's name in vain. Because we think it only has to do with vulgarity, we think we sidestep this issue with "gosh dangs." If we realized it also included our words and actions performed "in the name of Jesus," we might feel more needed tension and conviction.

Words Matter

There is no doubt that I have described someone as a "good kid" throughout the two decades I spent working with teenagers and their families. When we say someone is a good kid, we assign a value to them that places them on the more favorable spectrum between good and bad. We should never think to call any child a bad kid. The problem with these terms is the implied permanence of them.

Most things we describe in life as good or bad are static, or eventually end up being bad. Fleetwood Mac's *Rumours,* A Tribe Called Quest's *Low End Theory*, and REM's *Automatic for the People* are good albums. They will never stop being good albums. In contrast, the bunch of bananas you put in your shopping cart are only good until somewhere around the drive home, then they are bad. You tell yourself they are now good for banana bread or a smoothie so you place them in a Ziploc bag and put them in the freezer believing they will find redemption, but they won't. They will spend several months being forgotten and their tears will freeze into small icy shards covering them, protecting them from your betrayal. But one day you will tire of how their lumpy form keeps the pizzas from lying flat in the freezer drawer and you will finally throw them away. Because they're bad. All bad things get tossed out and often replaced.

A more relevant and accurate way to describe a kid (and any person for that matter) is to understand that we all exist on a sliding scale of health and unhealth. When a kid lacks the leadership, support, and accountability that healthy kids benefit from, they become unhealthy. They make poor choices. Even if they know the difference between right and wrong, they lack the health of perspective and many other tools to say the right thing or do the right thing.

A young man I met several years ago after moving to Waco comes to mind when thinking about this principle. Matt was one of the best skaters in town. He dominated street spots downtown as well as the city's public park. On most days, you could pass the skate park on Waco Drive and see Matt making tricks few other skaters could on the ledges, handrails, and down the stair sets. Skating seemed to come easy to Matt, but few other things in life did.

He struggled with methamphetamines and there was a lot of unhealth in and around his daily life. For the first few months of knowing him, I'd see Matt at the skate park with a backpack full of all his earthly belongings which amounted to a change of clothes, a bottle of Gatorade, and some cigarettes.

Matt gladly accepted any skate equipment I gave him. As much as he skated, his shoes and his boards were constantly falling apart, and he lacked the resources to replace them. I soon found myself giving Matt Middleman boards, buying him food, and giving him rides as he bounced from couch to couch in Waco. He applied to several fast-food jobs to get some consistency and income, but there was always a reason why he couldn't stick with it.

While our work at Middleman often looks like giving young men like Matt resources, encouragement, a healthy life example to follow, and even part-time work, there are times when the best thing we can do is help them move away from some of the negative influences that keep them from health. In Matt's case, he was able to move up north and live with extended family as he tried to better himself.

I saw Matt a year ago when he moved back down to Waco.

He told me he was a new dad and his son was beautiful but that the baby's mother had been unfaithful and they had separated. I asked if there was anything I could do for him, and he said he was hungry so we fed him and prayed for him; that God would reconcile his family and provide for them.

As much as I want to report that Matt and many others that we invest in are "success stories" who respond to God's love for them, accept Jesus, and go onto becoming missionaries, that does not happen often. Many of these young people never break the cycle of unhealth they were raised in.

They are not bad kids because there is no such thing as a bad kid.

They are unhealthy kids.

And what's the best thing about understanding the difference between health and unhealth? The fact that there are quality agents of change that can be applied to transform unhealth into health once more. Unhealth is temporary and even things unseen are fighting to be healthy and regenerative.

When I was a kid, I broke the poorly made key off in the lock of a cedar chest in my room. I attempted to "pick" the lock or fish the key out of it with a very sharp pocketknife. By applying great pressure to the knife, I successfully closed the blade back toward the handle with my left forefinger in the way to catch the blade. Forty years later, I have a prominent scar from the injury and next to my cuticle, a small piece of skin constantly regenerates and, because I'm gross, I pick at the skin once it's presented enough to grab with my teeth and then I spit it across the room if I'm indoors. It's one of the small ways my body shows that its working to reconcile, connect, and fight toward health.

Seeing a person as unhealthy instead of bad can be easier said than done. It takes patience, practice, and perspective. Oh, it also takes understanding, forming, and spending margin. Let's talk about that.

Margin is a Beautiful Thing

One of the best things our kids and mentees can learn from us is the theology of margin. We were first introduced to "margins" on lined notebook paper. If you were like me, you were taught to keep your work within the margins. They were to be our starting point and ending point for all the words and numbers we would fill our assignments with. The margins were important because they gave our teachers space to make corrections and leave notes.

The older I get the more I see the importance of creating and cultivating margins in our life. Without margin, we are prone to focus on surviving on a basic level as opposed to thriving at a higher one. Think of it this way, margins are the excess. Some people have excess money and so they can be generous with giving some to others. Some people have time so they spend it investing in others by calling them, visiting them, sitting with them to hear about their day and offering advice when its needed.

Freely You Have Been Given. Freely Give.

One of the most substantial passages of scripture that helps to explain the theology of margin is Matthew 10:7-8. This chapter starts off with Jesus calling all his closest friends together and he gives them power to cast out demons and heal sick people.

Matthew 9 lists several instances of Jesus' power and compassion. He heals the paralytic. He tells Matthew to become one of his disciples. He teaches about fasting. He goes to bring a little girl back to life and on the way heals a bleeding woman. He then raises the girl back to life by taking hold of her hand. He heals two blind men. He casts a demon out of a muted man.

The chapter ends with noting that Jesus had compassion on the harassed and helpless multitudes who followed him in hopes of finding healing and hope for themselves or their loved ones. He teaches about the harvest and the workers telling his friends that the work is overwhelming and nonstop so pray that more will be added to the workforce.

The very next chapter tells us that Jesus called his friends together and sent them out. It says he blessed them with the power to heal disease and drive out the presence of evil. Jesus tells his friends to go to the Jews exclusively, tell them that the Kingdom is near, and that they will heal the sick, clean up the lepers, and drive away every demon they come across.

It's like Jesus had just gotten his team together and was sending them on a short-term mission trip so they would understand this next chapter of their lives wasn't going to be about enjoying the marvels of being on a holy entourage where the leaders would do and say dynamic things. They had not been called to be spectators but instead activists for righteousness in God's name and that it would begin with:

1. A specific people and place to go to (people)
2. A message of hope, love, and urgency (proclamation)
3. A responsibility to act in obedience (productivity)

And then Jesus gives a practical instruction that informs our theology and has so moved my own thinking that I've printed it on hundreds of t-shirts and two vans (so far). He tells his friends that just as they *have been freely given, so should they freely give.*

God has freely given to you everything you have. He gave you your eye color just as he gave you the last breath you took. It was He who has given you everything in this world that you have worked so hard for just as He will continue to meet your every need out of the riches of his glory (Phil 4:19).

This statement is as perfectly logical as it is revolutionary. It is as simple to understand as it is incredibly complicated to exercise. You and I stumble with the idea and, most importantly, the application of being freely given to so that we may freely give daily.

Jesus knew this concept was outside the scope of his friends' understanding and practice, so he goes on to tell them they are to take no money or precious metals with them to trade for food, drink, or shelter. He tells them to pack no bags with extra clothes or toiletries. Jesus tells his friends they are to stay with people who will welcome and house them. He says that the folks who accept them will be blessed while those who don't will be cursed.

Jesus tells his representatives to live in the moment and use their discernment. He tells them that situations are going to get sticky, and they will be tempted to lean on their own understanding but that there won't be a need to come up with a quick answer or a way to get out of a ticket. Jesus tells them that God will, even in those moments, provide the words they are to say. Freely they will be given as the Spirit will freely speak through them.

The parallelism between the instructions Jesus gives his friends and his own ministry cannot be overlooked: Jesus came to a specific people (the Israelites) with a specific message (I Am) and with a specific job to do (bring life to the dead through the cross). Let's also cut to the chase here and say that these three sections are relevant to our own lives today as parents, mentors, and teachers.

We have relationships (people), have been given a message (proclamation), and have a job to do (productivity). Our words and actions should bless all people. Imagine living every day with that kind of purpose, knowing that God has planned for every conversation we are to have that will enlighten and encourage the people in our lives, everyone from your dearest family member to every stranger you encounter on the street.

Consider God freely giving to us so that we can freely give. This balanced instruction is incredible because we are told that the only reason we can be of any use to anybody out there is because God has equipped us so well for the job. But beyond that, we understand that anything that we give to someone else wasn't ours to begin with as it was only God's. So, I don't have to live my life in fear of someone taking something from me when I understand that anything I have was actually God's in the first place.

Sixpence None the Richer is one of my favorite bands that play Jesus music. The origin of their name has been well-documented as they were asked countless times to share what the name means. After performing their single, "Kiss Me" on Letterman in 1999, singer Leigh Nash got the chance to explain the name's meaning: "It comes from a book by C. S. Lewis called *Mere Christianity*. A little boy asks his father if he can get a sixpence—a very small amount of English currency—to go and get a gift for his father. The father gladly accepts the gift and he's really happy with it, but he also realizes that he's not any richer for the transaction. C.S. Lewis was comparing that to his belief that God has given him, and us, the gifts that we possess, and to serve him the way we should, we should do it humbly, with humble hearts—realizing how we got the gifts in the first place."

To FREELY give, we need to understand that everything that we have ever been given is not just from the Father, but that He still owns these things. We are simply blessed by them temporarily.

(Now go listen to *The Fatherless and the Widow* album by Sixpence None the Richer)

This is one of the lessons Jesus was teaching his friends as he gave them a people to go to, a message to share, and a job to get done. It was essential they understand that God was going before them so there would be no confusion of glory once they began to see lives changed when they went, spoke, and worked. He also told them to take no bags and extra clothes with them since God would also provide for their physical needs throughout the journey.

Many of us feel more loved by God because of all the things He gives us when it may be easier to hear His voice and see His direction when we aren't so preoccupied by all the stuff we choose to purchase and manage (or rather, be managed by) daily.

The Paradox of Self-Denial

What does the notion of self-denial mean to you? Does it conjure up mental images of denying yourself dessert in the name of good health? Does it make you think of a hard enduring of practices that are good for you but make you kind of miserable at the same time? Maybe you know enough about scripture to realize that present hardships will someday be followed by future glories and to stress the pay-off we probably need to go through some junk in the here and now. Indeed, Jesus said we will have hardships in this life but that we can take to heart that he overcame the very world that seems at times to be beating us down.

One of the many great lessons Jesus taught was that living in truth involves no longer living a lie. For many of the young people we serve and lead, the lie that they don't matter is overwhelming. In the next chapter we are going to shine a light on the issue of fear. It's no mistake that when God calls us to know Him and walk with Him, the first step involves turning from old ways so we can discover who we really are. Want to find yourself? Lose yourself. That old way of living can't be relied on to reveal your true identity. It can't point you toward your excellent purpose. It wasn't designed to equip you with a community to bless and be blessed by.

In the eternal words of Public Enemy, "you can't truss it."

CHAPTER 5

I'M NOT AFRAID

(Purpose is Identity on Wheels)

I'm afraid of driving over 65
I'm afraid of flying in the sky
I'm afraid of getting out of bed with nowhere to put my head
I'm afraid of multiple choice
When a and b and c and d are true
I'm afraid of not being afraid
-from Fleming and John's "I'm Not Afraid"

For as long as there has been effective marketing, the greatest consumer motivation and deterrent for decision making has been fear. Fear has many faces. The fear of "but, what if..." drives us to buy insurance in its many forms for our bodies and our most prized possessions. The fear of making mistakes (thereby revealing the very humanity we try so desperately to hide) leads us to make all kinds of decisions with safety in mind, even if we're miserable while being so safe. We are afraid of missing out on things, or even having to wait for them, so we buy things on credit. We're even so fearful of being alone that we settle and commit ourselves to people who abuse or take us for granted.

At its lowest common denominator, we can begin to understand fear as nothing more than a forced yielding. When we were young and afraid of the dark, we stopped before walking into the dark room (or crawling under the dark house, *aye dios mio*!) That kind of fear was especially potent because we put our bodies in an environment where our minds were free to wander and create all the many monsters lurking unseen that surely wanted to harm us. Once a light was turned on, the creature in the corner went back to being a coat on a hook (just as the night's headless "Memphis Man" of Lubbock spends his time in the sun as an electrical box attached to a telephone pole).

One of the greatest ways to overcome fear is to consider the realistic effects of disaster and pinpoint what we are truly afraid of. In other words, it's always best to shine a light on the matter. My career in youth ministry can be divided into two chapters separated by a pivotal moment in leadership of absolute and utter fear.

"I Think I Killed Phoebe and a Girl named Summer"

It had been a successful Super Week at Graceview Baptist in Tomball. For lack of a better description, Super Week was like Vacation Bible School for teenagers but instead of deeply spiritual exercises, activities included feats of resilience like let's have leaders each drink a gallon of whole milk in about ten minutes and then film what happens next.

That summer, I and my interns were excited about the purchase of a large pneumatic "earth ball" which, when fully inflated, stood a whopping six feet in diameter. We had several large-group games with the ball planned for the 100+ students who would be cramming our sanctuary-turned-gymnasium-for-the-week with lots of energy and fun throughout.

One of the games we planned for that evening started with the large ball sitting at halfcourt. Each of the four sides of the gym floor would be occupied by one of the four teams of thirty or so teenagers from each of the four teams. We assigned each player on each team a number and when we called out that number, that person would run to the corner of the gym and on our mark, they would run at full speed at the ball and then attempt to force the ball over any one of the other three teams' players while defending their own perimeter and then receive a point.

(Now, this is where I tell you about my pivotal moment in church leadership. I never remember asking before the "incident" if there was any way that someone could get greatly injured if a worse-case scenario took place through the course of a game we created. After what I'm about to describe took place, I never planned another activity for teenagers without asking this question.)

I am assuming that the potentially savage nature of this game led us to at least make sure that each battle would include four guys or four girls but never mixed. Someone called out a number and Karima, Courtney, Phoebe, and a visiting friend named Summer bound over to their respective corners and made themselves ready for the match.

A whistle was blown, and they were all off the line like a powder keg heading in a flash toward the huge ball and directly toward each other. And then the worst thing that could happen happened. Courtney had the other three girls beat by enough time to get herself and the ball completely out of the center court circle, but it happened much too quickly for Phoebe and Summer, who were running at full speed directly at each other, to do anything else but keep that pace. Time slowed to a crawl in my mind as I watched the two teenagers miss each other's hands completely and catch each other in the face, spin around a half turn, and fall on their backs in the same direction they were going before the collision. I was just feet away from the collision. It was brutal. I can still see the lights dim in Phoebe's eyes as her face turned toward me and her body fell away like Hans Gruber falling 30 floors down in *Die Hard*.

As you can imagine, the air was immediately sucked out of the room as all fell quiet and adult leaders ran over to the girls to check on them. Once I could leave them in the care of our leaders, I was outside the church building calling 911 for an ambulance. The next call was to each girl's parents followed by a call to my pastor to tell him what had happened and what we were doing about it.

And the last call I made was to Mandi.

I can't remember exactly what I told her because it was the first moment I had to start processing what had just happened and that was mixed with the flood of emotions you feel when sharing a traumatic experience in a safe space with a trusted loved one. I was so afraid that I was responsible for permanent damage to these two young girls.

The girls and their families went immediately to the emergency room and our program leaders met up with them later. I was relieved beyond measure when I walked into the waiting room to see Phoebe and Summer laughing with friends and family. Phoebe had a large bandage on her forehead and Summer was sporting two black eyes. I spent the rest of the night apologizing to the girls and their parents. They were gracious and forgiving, knowing that accidents happen.

I started planning events much more like a dad after that night for fear that something like that would ever happen again.

Deciding to Do Things Poorly

I grew up in the age of the heroic youth minister. When I was a teenager, those guys were incredible athletes, excellent musicians, socially engaging conversationalists, and seasoned craftsmen presenting Bible studies on Wednesday nights. Once I started thinking that maybe I was supposed to go into youth ministry, I realized quickly that I didn't have the goods to become such a glossy and fine-tuned leader. So, I decided to go in the other direction. Instead of sharpening all my skills to convince everybody that I had it all together, I would lead by revealing my shortcomings and if church members or parents struggled with my blind spots, they could find their place to bridge that gap and make the youth ministry that much better. I'm thankful it worked.

I can remember early on in my becoming a professional Christian, that my mentor, captain, and inspiration, Troy Sikes, shared two truths with me: don't neglect your home for the sake of leading within the church, and ministry is more of a marathon than it is a sprint. I took his words to heart, and they still shape my leadership approach. I share these truths with young pastors I work with today.

Troy was my youth minister growing up and I was fortunate enough to reconnect with him when I moved to Lubbock to go to Tech. One day over tacos he asked, "What if we built a skate park in our church parking lot?" And so began the process of pooling a team of skaters and builders together that would result in CheapSkate, a free modular skate park offered to the skaters, bikers, and inline skaters in Lubbock, TX. Over the span of almost a year we got to see 200 teenagers register with our ministry and averaged about 75 of them in attendance every week.

The game plan was simple: get up very early on Saturday and drag skate ramps and obstacles onto the parking lot from the storage room behind the Activity Building. Skaters would ride from sunup to sundown and leaders would take opportunities throughout the day to have conversations with teenagers. We learned their names and asked them what life was like. We asked if we could pray for them and shared with them what we knew about who God is and what He has to offer. Rarely did we ever take the approach of having everyone sit down to hear the Gospel from a speaker but there were times it happened. Mostly our approach was to connect in a smaller way where we could have dialogue and ask them individually how we could support them and pray for them.

I am thankful for the sponsoring support of the church that allowed and even helped fund CheapSkate. When I left Lubbock to start a career in youth ministry, we hadn't formed any enduring leadership for CheapSkate, so the ministry quickly dissolved. That was a substantial lesson in the difference between a church allowing a ministry and truly supporting it. I shoulder the blame as well since I took no steps to cultivate leadership of the ministry before leaving.

Several years later a group of youth ministry parents asked about the possibility of creating another skate ministry and I was apprehensive enough to say, "not unless we do it together." And so, Middleman Skate Park began with the same approach of dragging ramps out into the parking lot on a Saturday morning but quickly picked up enough steam to allow for the conversion of 2400 sq feet of church storage space in the bus barn to be designated as an indoor park comprised of six-foot and four-foot mini ramps and a small street course. We saw God work in amazing ways through the years at Middleman. He brought entire families into our church from Middleman being the first point of contact for their skateboarding kids. The Gospel was shared and accepted by many children and teenagers through conversations and events like our Saturday night skate nights and skate camps.

Grace Upon Grace

One of the greatest ministries spawning from Middleman Skate Park was the creation of Middleman Skateboards. One day my mother-in-law, who taught elementary music to children, asked if I had any ideas about how to deal with an unruly 3rd grader so I gave her a random skateboard deck left over from a contest at the skate park. She got back to me days later saying she gave the deck away to the kid and now he's her best friend.

It made sense that in gifting skateboarders with a piece of equipment you are not only validating the activity that they seldom get support for, you're also modeling God's grace in a very tangible way: giving something to them they didn't earn while asking nothing in return.

Since so much of skateboarding is graphic in nature, it made sense to create a brand that would be God-honoring but interesting enough to be less-obvious and not look like something hanging on the wall of a Christian bookstore. I bought ten poorly constructed skate decks off eBay for $10 each and began spray painting Middleman graphics. The more I gave away the more I found opportunities to naturally connect with skaters and share about who God is and what He had done in my life. Once I read "freely you have been given, freely give" in Matthew, I began getting friends to create art pieces that would become mantras for how we share the Gospel within Middleman.

Lawton

Lawton Outlaw was a skater a few years older than me. He went to Dobie High School which I thought meant he could afford to buy new skateboards and probably didn't have to duct tape his shoes together. Being a friend of Mandi's family, he attended our wedding years later. He lived in LA and looked cool, like a member of the band, The Cult. These were my only points of reference about Lawton before getting a message one day from him in 2010. Just days before reaching out to me he posted about starting to connect with teenagers at the public skate park in downtown Houston. My brother-in-law told him he should contact me.

At that time, I was producing two Middleman Skateboard graphics and some basic logo shirts. It was a one-man show. It didn't take long before Lawton's initiative and excitement began improving the ministry at every level. He is an incredibly talented graphic designer who loves music, skateboarding, and motorcycles. Our connecting couldn't have been at a better time in both our lives. I was coasting in some ways, and he needed to join something larger than himself that would give him some added credibility and reference at the skate park. In other words, representing a skate company at the park while you are gaining relationship as a mentor to skaters is much easier than being a random 40-year-old man out there trying to strike up conversations with teenagers.

I will always consider Lawton the Chuck Yeager of Middleman. He was our test pilot who took conceptual ministry ideas and applied them to his skate community in real time. With his background in business, we created the needed components of the organization. We worked together to form things like a mission statement and core values. Lawton designed a ministry prospectus which told the Middleman story. We even started collaborating on graphic ideas that would strengthen the aesthetic of the "brand" while also sharpening our organizational culture and language. One of the greatest achievements during this exciting time of the ministry was working to produce the Middleman Mentor Bible which includes a custom cover and message inside the jacket. (If you need any proof that Middleman is very much an analog ministry living in a digital world just look to the fact that we began investing time and resources into printing hundreds of paper bibles instead of building a strong social media presence or designing an app. We're grumpy old men.)

Lawton and his wife, Chrissy, plugged themselves into the lives of skaters at the downtown park. They invested in them, invited them to church, introduced them to Jesus as Lord, and encouraged them in quality discipleship. While it was a blessing to see Lawton flesh-out concepts concerning graphic and over-all ministry development, it was even more gratifying to watch him make Middleman so much better with his fresh ideas and openness to the Lord. One tool that Lawton created while working as a Middleman Mentor is something that speaks into our ministry philosophy and is something we still use today.

Our mentor "business card" is a die cut sticker of our logo. Sharing our stickers with kids gives us a chance to tell part of the Middleman story through explaining what the name means (spoiler alert, it's Jesus) and asking if they see the cross in our logo. More times than not they will say "no" so we point it out as being a void between the two Ms. I always like when somebody then says, "oooooh." Once a person sees the cross, they can't unsee it. However, we don't lead with a "turn or burn" kind of message. Our job is not to frighten or pressure a person into knowing that God loves them. Instead, we serve by offering the ministry of accessibility.

We want skaters to know God loves them and they don't have to live life alone. We print the ministry website, social media info, and our personal phone number on the back of our stickers. The idea was Lawton's brainchild and one that we encourage other ministries to do as well. We've gotten texts in the middle of the night when a teenager is struggling and needs to know that someone is out there who cares for them and wants them to be well.

Lawton sustained a few injuries while skating that made it difficult to ride the burly pools at his concrete park. God was beginning to give him a heart for the motorcycle community in Houston, so he traded four wheels for two bigger (and faster) ones. He is still a dear friend of mine and I look back at all the things we built together with a full and thankful heart. You can bet your bottom dollar he's somewhere in Houston riding a Ducati right now.

Perfecting the Practice of Doing Things Poorly

As my leadership style of "great idea, poor execution" grew, I was not only unafraid of doing things badly, but I was also doing it more and more. The lesson was mostly learned within car and home remodel projects. Some people are good at researching things and knowing what tools are needed for a job, how long the job should take, and what other resources and options are included in the project. That's not me. I'm better at ripping into a thing, seeing how it works (or why it doesn't), and then coming up with a plan. The good part of this is that there's no paralysis by over analysis. The bad part is that it probably takes a lot longer than it should have AND I might work myself into a predicament that requires help from someone else.

And there lies the gold.

Pulling people into our projects and ideas is where the good stuff happens.

Our first two kids were two and less than a year old when we moved to Brenham, TX. Since I worked so close to home, I thought I could get away with buying a project vehicle for a daily driver. I don't recommend this but how often are we willing to put ourselves through what we would never wish for anyone else?

At that time, the primary place to find jalopies was Craigslist. After some scanning I found a 1971 GMC 1500 long bed pickup in Marble Falls. It ran and stopped and was listed for $1,500. It wasn't long before Mandi, the kids, and I were on the road to bring back what would certainly become the pride of the Brenham roads! The thing to remember about buying cars that you first see online is that things look so much better in the pics than when you see the car in person. This particular truck had been near a fire at some point in its life, so the turn signal lenses were melted, the headlights cracked and cloudy, and most of the windshield was a spiderweb of cracks making it almost impossible to see out of. So, I offered $1,400 and soon found myself driving back to Brenham looking out the small patch of clear windshield with Mandi and the kids behind me in the dependable station wagon.

That day was the first of many drives that I would take in which I would ask God to bless my ignorance and supernaturally allow a vehicle I was driving to reach its destination safely. There are still many days that I drive a project car and can only point to God's grace for the successful travel.

The next morning after bringing my truck home – it wouldn't start. And so began the parts throwing. The next "lightbulb" moment of my life came during the days of restoring my GMC in the driveway. One of the best parts of that project was asking my friend Todd to mill some boards that I could use as planks for the bed. The original boards in the truck were long gone after deteriorating over time but the metal strips that held them down were still in place. It wasn't long before Todd had milled some aged cypress planks ready to cut, sand, route, stain, and install.

I don't think you can do any better than an old truck if you are interested in learning about restoration and basic mechanic work. The room under the hood makes for easy part swapping and upgrades and I've never had a hard time selling a truck in Texas. Because trucks have always been popular and there were so many produced each year, there is an excellent aftermarket for them which means that companies exist that produce any part you will ever need for most American models.

One day a teenager at my church asked if he could come over the next time I was working on the truck because he didn't know much about mechanic stuff and wanted some exposure to engine work. Next on the list for the GMC was to replace some gaskets to eliminate the oil puddles in the driveway. Scott came over and helped replace the valve cover and oil pan gaskets.

Later that evening, I was thinking about how good it was to have help with the truck and talk about some life stuff with Scott as we worked. He enjoyed the chance to learn something new about how engines work and to invest his time into my truck while feeling the satisfaction of a job well done. Why was my truck no longer going to leak oil? Because he fixed it.

I repeated this methodology in youth ministry shortly thereafter when our youth group invested in a 1963 bread van. The idea was simple: buy a unique vehicle that the youth group could learn on as they invested their time into the project. They could also help bring other community members into the mix by requesting discounts from local tire shops and mechanics. Since most of the work could be done inhouse, we recruited some of the older men from our church to fix things and teach the teenagers as well. Once the van was ready, we had a church member trailer it to College

Station for fresh paint and had a local sign company make us custom vinyl stickers for the huge side panels. Since Brenham is a small Texas town with a historic downtown, the city holds several parades each year and always has a huge turnout for the Friday night football game at the high school. We took advantage of these opportunities by running the van through as many parades as possible with our teenagers walking alongside it and we tailgated out of the van before every home game outside the main gates so we could greet and offer free hotdogs and snow cones to all game attenders as they walked by.

We lived in Brenham for five years and then spent another six years in Bellville (twenty minutes down the highway.) The youth group "mascot" vehicle was such a success that we repeated the process in Bellville, but this time we purchased an incredibly solid and all-original 1971 GMC ¾ ton long bed from long-time friends and Middleman supporters, the Galloway family. As my cousin Brad likes to say, "You can take those trucks completely apart with one 9/16-inch socket wrench." He's not wrong. That's pretty much what we did. We had a solid group of teenagers in Bellville who worked to disassemble, soda blast, and sand down that entire truck. A professional painter came in and made a makeshift paint bay out of a church member's garage and before we knew it, the once blue truck was silver to match the Bellville Brahma football helmets. We finished the truck off with red and white racing stripes (also just like the helmets) and our youth group logo on the hood and rear quarter panels. The Bellville truck turned out so nice that we featured it in several car shows during my time there.

While we built both vehicles with student, church member, and community involvement, like many things, their potential and use waned when new leadership took over in both ministries. Thankfully, we had invested less into each of these projects than they were worth so the van and truck would later be sold for more than was spent on them.

The practice of doing things poorly so that others can join the team went to another level when my friend, Marsha, recommended that we elevate Middleman to official non-profit status instead of continuing to do it as a guy out of my garage.

Going Legit and Forming a Board.

Another development during the time God was teaching us about skate ministry through Lawton's work in Houston was the formation of a board of directors. I didn't intend for Middleman to grow outside of it being a small way to bless skaters and share my faith. Something cool happened the longer we went – others bought in.

Forming a nonprofit can be tricky. The advantages are huge as you benefit from establishing yourself as a federally recognized entity, you become legitimate to potential donors and supporters, and it helps sharpen your organization's vision and mission. As much as I would like to share the step-by-step process of how we formed our 501C3, Marsha Gosney took care of all the paperwork to get our nonprofit status and it only took us four months from start to finish.

One integral part of solidifying Middleman as a nonprofit was forming a board of directors who act as decision makers, sounding boards, and praying confidants. Our original three board members were Lawton, Marsha, and me. We were soon able to get a trusted mentor of mine, John Eckeberger, to agree to join the team and we then added Greg Elliott, who Lawton had known at the downtown skate park. John's involvement was key as he had so much ministry experience from working as a youth pastor to a church planter and entrepreneur. John was my youth minister, Troy's, youth minister. He always brings a focused and wise perspective into an issue. Greg is our finance and leadership guy who is as easy to talk to as he is committed to serving the Lord. I go to him a lot for leadership perspective and problem solving. Our most-recent board member is my good friend, John Newberry. I met John twenty years ago when he was heading up a skate ministry in Austin. He is my go-to when I need some general encouragement (or as Tyler Childers would say, "when my feet hang low.")

When it comes to forming a board or any kind of team, I highly recommend valuing diversity of perspectives and personalities over ease. Let's be honest, some people are just easier than others. Throughout my years in ministry and leadership, I've seen a natural tendency for many people to surround themselves with people. Just. Like. Them. Why is this such an easy pitfall to stumble into? Because life and ministry are hard. It makes total sense that you would want a team of people who "get you" and who you don't struggle to communicate with.

The major issue with this approach to leadership is blind spots. The same type of person is going to see a problem or opportunity from the same vantage point thus come up with the same solution! When it comes to forming your team, look for agreement in the non-negotiables but look for differences in personalities, experiences, and perspectives. These differences will serve the organization well, ensure that you remain intentional in your leadership, and challenge everyone further into effectiveness.

While differences are important and ease of communication is valuable, one factor you want to strive for within your organization's leadership team is TRUST. As you already know, trust can take forever to build and just a moment to destroy. I had a luxury in thinking about who would make a "dream team" since I had so many years in ministry (one advantage of being old). I knew I could trust all my board members to be people of integrity who understood Middleman's purpose and personality. Their experience and perspective would prove essential during the next chapter of Middleman.

How a Lack of Purpose Develops a Lack of Hope

An old analogy used to describe the power of hope involves a prison yard. For a guard to break the spirit of a prisoner, all he must do is start by having him spend an entire day moving an enormous pile of rocks from one area of the yard to another on Monday. While the prisoner may be dehydrated and exhausted, barely even able to walk or think straight, he can at least look back on the day's work with some sense of pride and accomplishment. Then on Tuesday, the guard forces the prisoner to put all the rocks back in their original place. He repeats the process for as many days as it takes for the prisoner to realize his hard work is pointless and without purpose.

While many of us feel the same way about doing laundry or making our beds each morning, the point is that without a clear and distinct purpose, we can easily begin to lose a sense of hope for the future. And hope, by definition, is the ability to rise above our circumstances to know that even though things are at their worst, there will come a time that the light will pierce the darkness and peace and prosperity will return. Even with a strong sense of identity, an unexercised purpose leaves us wanting.

Of all the things they can be known for, Christians should be characterized by their practice of prayer and their unfazed priority of hope. The writer of Hebrews tells us that our faith is being sure of what we hope for and certain of what we can't see. It's realizing that God is in the constant work of connecting and reconnecting His creation in many ways.

CHAPTER 6

IMAGINATION

(Purpose Develops Over Time)

Imagination is funny
It makes a cloudy day sunny
Makes a bee think of honey
Just as I think of you
Imagination is crazy
Your whole perspective gets hazy
Starts you asking a daisy
What to do, what to do
-from Frank Sinatra's "Imagination"

As I mentioned in the introduction, while teaching innovative or artistic concepts that have proved helpful in ministry, I've had people in the room label themselves as not being "a creative." They weren't refusing to recognize that they lacked creativity as an attribute, they were saying their identity was that *not of a creative*!

A quick showing of hands:
Who on earth wasn't created by a creative Creator?
Who has yet to experience laughter?
Who has never eaten a taco and found it delicious?

Anyone who couldn't raise her hand to at least one of these questions has a right to say she is not a "creative."

The rest of us have no excuse.

While the attribute may go unrealized, unexperienced, and underappreciated, that is not to say it's not there.

It's odd how the word "imagination" goes so unused in the church. For fear of straying from a narrower view of reality, we must think there is no place for it. We probably mistrust it. Maybe we even fear it. Ok, maybe you find it on the wall in the children's ministry...

Theologian Kevin Vanhoozer says the modern church suffers from "imaginative malnutrition." We find ourselves at an unprecedented place in history. Western Christians have enjoyed centuries of a privileged place in society, but now we struggle to engage a society that doesn't recognize or respect faith, theological convictions, and status of clergy as in past generations. Times like these require heavy doses of imagination and creativity, but sadly, for decades now creatives and artists have not been given a voice in church leadership circles. The decision-making leadership roles have gone to CEO-mimicking leaders and guardians of doctrine — the "priests" of the faith community, relegating the spontaneous, the new, the unfamiliar — the "prophetic," to secondary, non-executive, but often non-existent roles.

Trends common in the church are typically mirrored in our homes. Spiritual growth and development priorities neatly confined to religious practices and redundancies that choke out imagination offer a safe predictability. It reminds me of a good friend who gave up on the church as an eighth grader when his earnest questions about faith were discouraged by a Sunday School teacher unwilling to sway from the morning's lesson. The teacher believed man was made for the sabbath, I suppose.

One thing I like about life is discovering and learning how to do things. As a metaphor, I'd like to have as many tools in my toolbox as possible. This has led me to practice construction and repair while understanding engineering. It has fueled my interest in relationship dynamics and how to understand and express emotion. I'm not saying I'm good at any of those things, in fact, remember I'm the "good idea, bad execution" guy.

But we are hamstrung as a created people when, in our quest to understand the very definition of who we are and practice the act of what we're supposed to be doing, we neglect the incredible ability we have in letting our minds think beyond that which our eyes take in.

Let's put some handlebars on this idea.

Some questions to consider as you evaluate how creative your daily environment is for yourself and your kids:

- Is music played in your home or car throughout the course of the day?
- Are any original art pieces hanging on your walls?
- Does your family talk about movies after you watch them together?
- Do your kids have access to musical instruments in your home?
- Do you have any family traditions that involve creativity or imagination?
- Does your family ever try different types of food for supper?
- Is there a craft area in your home?
- Do your young children have a chest full of old Halloween costumes and play clothes?

- Do your kids help decorate your home for different holidays?

You may not see much value in developing or applying your imagination to learning from Scripture or growing your faith. Chances are, if you don't see it as a priority for yourself, you will struggle to prioritize it for someone you influence. But exercising your imagination as a facility and seeing it as useful can be hugely satisfying and can deepen your faith as you live purposefully.

Dropping the Screw

I met Ronnie Marshall in 2011 when we moved to Bellville, Texas after accepting a job at First Baptist Church. Ronnie was a machinist, builder, and mechanic who was kind and supportive and always hugged lots of people. Ronnie spoke with a slow Texas drawl and wore a constant smile on his face. Once I realized Ronnie possessed a very particular set of skills, skills he had acquired over a very long career... I started asking him questions about the 1971 GMC ¾ ton pick up our youth group had purchased and started working on to get running. Ronnie was the guy who showed me how to check compression on a motor by using your thumb. He was also the only man I knew that, in earnest, would stop and pray for the location of a screw or a washer once it fell into an engine bay.

Take a minute and think about this for a second: you're working under a hood, removing parts, and dealing with small, greasy screws and nuts, and suddenly, that manifold screw slips out of your fingertips and into the shadowy abyss of the lower engine area. Your first impulse is definitely to cuss a little. Of course, as soon as it left your fingers you held your breath and listened intently at all the cascading sounds of metal on metal in hopes that it will make its way all the way to concrete. It seems like an eternity and you know the bolt now exists in the fourth dimension where socks from the dryer and the good steak knives from the drawer go to live for eternity.

The time it happened with Ronnie Marshall, I remember him saying, "Well John, what I like to do when this happens is pray." And he did. Ronnie prayed for our time together and the project and that the Lord would show us quickly exactly where that screw dropped because the truck was God's truck and it was God's screw that we dropped.

After the prayer, we found the screw.

I told Ronnie that I usually don't find the screw. He stopped smiling and set the wrench down. His eyes held serious intention as they met mine. He said every time he has prayed to find a small car part that slips from his hand, he's found it. The weight of his tone had little to do with a piece of metal. It was more about the need for us to remember that God is present in our day-to-day trivial tasks just as He is in our glorious mountaintop experiences and our valley-of-death trials.

Whenever I am under the hood of a car and I drop a small part into the darkness of the motor, Ronnie's smiling face pops into my mind (and that helps because it deflects my silent cussing in the moment). The second thought I have is my need to go directly to God to pray for that little piece of threaded metal that slipped away. I ask God to calm my heart, open my eyes, and show me where that thing is so I can finish the job.

I can tell you with 100% honesty and accuracy exactly

how many times I have failed to find the lost part since Ronnie Marshall showed me how to pray over it.

Zero.

So, what can you learn from Ronnie Marshall? Maybe it's relearning some basic theological truths. Maybe it's learning some for the first time. I hope it's at least to know that purposeful prayer works, and it's meant for all of life's little situations, very much so when it comes to parenting, teaching, and investing in the lives of others. Ronnie reminded me that all things, even dropped screws, matter and that all things are connected.

All Things Connected

I would warn anyone to avoid an ideology or religion that struggles to connect Creation. It's like David as he writes a love song to God in Psalm 139:

You have searched me, Lord,
and you know me.
2 You know when I sit and when I rise;
you perceive my thoughts from afar.
3 You discern my going out and my lying down;
you are familiar with all my ways.
4 Before a word is on my tongue
you, Lord, know it completely.
5 You hem me in behind and before,
and you lay your hand upon me.
6 Such knowledge is too wonderful for me,
too lofty for me to attain.
7 Where can I go from your Spirit?
Where can I flee from your presence?

8 If I go up to the heavens, you are there;
if I make my bed in the depths, you are there.
9 If I rise on the wings of the dawn,
if I settle on the far side of the sea,
10 even there your hand will guide me,
your right hand will hold me fast.
11 If I say, "Surely the darkness will hide me
and the light become night around me,"
12 even the darkness will not be dark to you;
the night will shine like the day,
for darkness is as light to you.
13 For you created my inmost being;
you knit me together in my mother's womb.
14 I praise you because I am fearfully and wonderfully made;
your works are wonderful,
I know that full well.
15 My frame was not hidden from you
when I was made in the secret place,
when I was woven together in the depths of the earth.
16 Your eyes saw my unformed body;
all the days ordained for me were written in your book
before one of them came to be.
17 How precious to me are your thoughts, God!
How vast is the sum of them!
18 Were I to count them,
they would outnumber the grains of sand—
when I awake, I am still with you.

It's all there, isn't it? This passage includes some bangers definitely worthy of some home décor plaques made out of shiplap and written in lively cursive at Hobby Lobby! In this, one of my favorite Psalms, David speaks to the omnipresence, omnipotence, and omniscience of a God that he can't even fully comprehend, yet fully enjoys.

But then he says this:

If only you, God, would slay the wicked!
Away from me, you who are bloodthirsty!
20 They speak of you with evil intent;
your adversaries misuse your name.
21 Do I not hate those who hate you, Lord,
and abhor those who are in rebellion against you?
22 I have nothing but hatred for them;
I count them my enemies.

That escalated quickly.

David goes from blowing kisses at God to spitting venom at his enemies. I think about this every time a "church" pickets against a people or an ignorant "pastor" speaks out against a type of person he struggles to understand or value. Psalm 139 is a great example of the human condition, that we have within us the ability to go immediately from worshipping God to missing the point altogether when considering those who God created in His image.

Had God smitten all who were against Him in that moment, you and I wouldn't be here now.

Scripture is littered with self-righteous men drawing lines in the sand in the name of God as they determine who is "in" and who is "out." Thankfully, David's emotions are resolved by his wisdom as He asks for sanctification:

Search me, God, and know my heart;
test me and know my anxious thoughts.

24 See if there is any offensive way in me,
and lead me in the way everlasting.

Oh, if this could be our real and practical prayer on a moment-by-moment basis. Hang those two verses on your wall, stitch them on a pillow, and tattoo them on your heart.

Proverbs 20:29

"It was the driver of the boat." That's always what any grown man tells me whenever I talk about how I'm no good at getting up and out of the water on a slalom ski or wake board. What they're saying is it's not because my arms are so skinny you can mistake one of them for a long string hanging from my sleeve, it's instead because whoever was throttling the boat pulling me wasn't doing it right. It's always very nice of them to deflect the blame like that.

In 2001, Mandi and I were waterskiing with friends on Lake Travis in Austin. The funniest thing happened in the middle of the day after everybody had turns behind the boat: I got tired. I had, of course, gotten tired many times before this moment, but that was the first time I had to stop doing something that I wanted to do because my body just couldn't go anymore. The exhaustion snuck up on me and rudely let me know that I was getting older. I was twenty-seven.

Proverbs 20:29 says that a young man's glory is in his strength and an old man's beauty is in his grey hair.

This verse almost reveals itself like a math equation. There is a symmetry and equal value between two different types of people, the young and the old. Both young and old enjoy substantial identity but their purpose is found in two different places. We also gather a logic from the verse as it can be used to speak of two separate people who live at the same time in history or one person transitioning from being young and then growing old.

When you are young, you are strong. You possess strength because your body is fresh and able. But you don't have wisdom because you have yet to acquire the knowledge and experience that combine to form it. As you age and your wisdom increases, your body's strength and ability decrease. But community gets a shout out in this verse as well because it reminds us that the young, though they are strong, desperately need older people in their lives showing them what it means to live rightly beyond their youthful ignorance. Our older generations benefit from young peoples' strength, and they can find the sweet spot in their lives once they are investing in young people as mentors, coaches, supporters, etc.

Without this perspective, we have the danger of young people who want so much to be adults they bypass the innocence and fun that should be part of growing up for the seriousness of staring into their phones all day as they fret over social media and yearn for dating relationships that go too far too fast in hopes of enjoying adult things before they are ready. There are also many grown adults who aren't ready to lose the benefits of youth, so they color the gray and dress as if they're thirty years younger. It's like spending the first half of your life wanting to be older only to spend the second half of your life wishing to be younger. The real problem is you never get to enjoy the contentment that comes with living where you are in the moment.

Purposeful living develops naturally over time as our strength may wain, but our wisdom should flourish. It makes sense that when we are young, we are 100% concerned about ourselves. Even with parents, mentors, and ministers investing in us, we remain in a state of soaking up as much attention and energy as possible, very rarely considering the notion that we can be rivers instead of lakes. It's what Richard Rohr calls the first half of our lives while we are constructing the container we will use during the second half of our lives as we live purposefully to serve others.

The issue for many is they never stop living from this first half of life source, so they never go onto live in the fullness that a seasoned purpose reveals to us. It's as if they omit the part when Jesus said that those coming after him must first deny themselves and take up their cross before they are freed up to follow him.

CHAPTER 7

LIFE AIN'T FAIR AND THE WORLD IS MEAN

(Purpose in Taking Up a Cross)

That's the way it goes in this day and age
Well, you ain't gotta read between the lines
You just gotta turn the page
Well, the most outlaw thing that I've ever done
was give a good woman a ring
And that's the way it goes
Life ain't fair and the world is mean
-from Sturgill Simpson's "Life Ain't Fair and the World is Mean"

Thankful for What Has Already Been Done Tomorrow

It all started with Mandi. She saw the incredible potential of Middleman (and my own lack of inspiration and excitement in my job at the time). While I would have told anybody in 2015 that doing Middleman full-time would be a dream, the "better safe than sorry" voice in my head kept telling me that a bird in the hand was much better than any amount in the bush. Up until that season in my life my MO had been to look back on past experiences and say, "God is good." In fact, I could easily see His hand in innumerable life circumstances but when considering the future with the same certainty? Nope.

I have exercised my faith often through the years. But the older I got, the more I saw leaders around me take safer bets. This is a universalism and a human tendency. Author and speaker, Francis Chan, has spoken over the tension between adventure and comfort several times (the idea may be included in one of his books). Simply put, Chan insists that mankind has not been created for comfort but adventure. The problem is we are prone to live in such a way as to find more ways of doing less. We buy insurance to give ourselves mental comfort if calamity happens. We buy homes and cars with more and more features which allow us to be more comfortable as we sleep, as we eat, as we shower, as we watch bigger, sharper TVs on bigger, softer couches, and "drive" cars that do all the driving for us. We can even get all our clothes, electronics, entertainment, and food streamed or delivered.

While the world believes the falsehood that "hard work's reward is comfort" the truth is "hard work's reward is more hard work." For one, hard work is a blessing with many benefits. (See Genesis 1) Work will never end but the type of work one does will. There was a time when I was no happier than to build a privacy fence for somebody. I could run a ten or twelve hour workday and get 300 feet of fencing up with a post in the ground every eight feet. But those days are over. Recently, I installed a gate at our house which required only three post holes dug 18 inches in the ground and by the end of the day I was ready for Jesus to just come and take me. Thankfully, as I prep for life as a 50-year-old, I get to experience the hard work of another kind – the kind that stresses my body less but my mind and attitude more as I work to equip and encourage folks who equip and encourage others.

In a real way, the Lord had been tilling the soil and prepping my heart through Mandi for what would come next. It seemed very out of the blue but, like all Godly things, it was in perfect timing.

The $80,000 Check that Never Got Deposited

I've known Michael Weaver since high school. We became friends as freshmen but my memory stakes more claims of him during our senior year. Michael and I habitually ditched Mrs. Fernandez's finance class and drove around with Harry Bigham wreaking minor havoc on the small businesses in South Houston, most of them drive thru attendant-related and none of which I am proud of. While our time together included bottles of Mad Dog and two liters of Purple Passion, I hadn't heard from Michael for nearly twenty years when he reached out on social media to say he was living in Brenham and could we meet for coffee.

We picked up where we left off (minus the under-age drinking and petty misdemeanors of our youth) and we started meeting together on a regular basis even after I moved to Bellville and Michael took a job as pastor at a small community church there. One day over coffee he asked, "What if our church supports you for a year while you take Middleman full-time?" The question felt heavy and confusing and freeing and practical all at the same time. As I took some days to think, pray, and talk about the idea with Mandi, God gave me a peace and excitement that I hadn't felt for some time. In a way, I was catching up to how she had felt for years about it.

When I took the idea to my board, there was a unanimous "YES." The next step in the full-time Middleman journey was to find out what this would look like.

"Skate ministry" is a broad and vague term. The obvious implication is that it will somehow serve and lead within the skateboarding community as a form of outreach, evangelism, and/or discipleship. Most skate ministries are volunteer-led entities that work independently or are attached to a larger church or parachurch group. These ministries center their efforts on one public skate park or maintain their own facilities. A few, like Middleman, are nonprofits which span state lines, maybe produce products, and work to grow a leadership team and donors across the nation and worldwide.

The next step for shifting Middleman into full-time ministry was to pray and fast over what the ministry was to look like and where we would live to lead the ministry. God revealed His plan for this just months before we would move from Bellville in 2016.

While still working at the church, I took students to Waco for a week of serving the city by partnering with Shepherds Heart Ministries. Two days into the trip, it was clear Waco could serve as MM headquarters. Being a college town, it had the influence and energy of a large state university. The Brazos River runs through the city and brings culture and appreciation. You don't have to travel far throughout Waco to see a socioeconomical and cultural diversity that is one of the city's strong suits. Waco has a long and difficult history that has left a residue in the traditions, values, and attitudes of its current residents.

One of the best things we discovered the city had going for it was (and is) its potential for involvement. In some ways, the city has just begun forming the identity it will continue to develop. Mandi and I moved to Austin in 1999. We moved there just weeks after she graduated from Tech with her undergrad and our getting married the next month in June. Our first home was a 800 sq foot apartment right off Ben White Blvd that cost us a whole $500 a month. We loved living near downtown Austin and how many different types of people called the city home. I see the same quality in Waco today.

Waco is geographically centered between cities that we maintain mentors in or need access to for programming. You don't have to travel more than five hours to reach as far as Lubbock and cities like San Antonio, Austin, Houston, and the Metroplex are all within three hours.

Once we got serious about moving to Waco, it was time to look for housing. The most substantial issue was I would be quitting an established career of twenty years to take on a position within an organization that had yet to support an employee. I wasn't just apprehensive about not finding a lender that would approve a home loan for us, I was gripped with fear over the matter.

In walks the peace of the Lord via Mandi's wisdom.

Within one of our tough conversations during that time, Mandi challenged me to reconsider one of my most-established theological practices (as I mentioned before) – the ability to look back on God's goodness and provision with confidence but the inability to do so while considering the future. One of the most important questions she's ever asked me helped shape my confidence to such a degree that it would go on to influence my decision-making for Middleman from that day forward:

"What if this is the time in your life when you realize that what God has in store for you in the future is as certain and established as what He's done for you in the past?"

Is that idea not the most scandalous thing you've ever heard? It was for me. Thankfully, she was correct and that truth allowed me to begin praying from a place of expectancy and gratitude. If this was God moving us on, then He would establish our feet every step of the way.

During that short season as we took idea and inspiration into action, I formed a stance of prayer and practice that I continue to think about and share through prayer often. What I'll do when led is to ask the Lord for His courage to remain where I should in a matter, not going out far ahead of His direction, and not lagging far behind, but instead remaining within His will, abiding in Him. The mental image of proximity to God is important for us because it speaks to the same issue King Saul displayed in his inability to obey God's direction. Like Saul, I can be overly ambitious for what I believe God will be happy with (or maybe even not care about so I can make it about me). In times like these, I run ahead of God's plan for me, from a sense that it either doesn't matter, that I have a better idea than what He has for me, or out of fear that I better get it now while the getting's good and maybe there won't be enough to go around later (see manna from heaven in Exodus 16).

I've never been accused of being the most ambitious knife in the drawer so I usually tend to sit back and do less than I should as opposed to doing more. So, when I pray for the sense to move forward when my wiring and my tendencies may say otherwise, the prayer stems from knowing myself and the need to rest in Him instead of on my laurels.

Armed with the promise of a year's worth of support

guaranteed with a handshake* and with the hope that we'd find a home in a new city, I told the good people at First Baptist Church Bellville that we'd be leaving in the fall. There was no turning back now.

Part of the moving process involved Mandi investing countless hours researching Waco real estate. One of the few house-touring trips we took during this time included a visit to N 27th St. The quarter-mile block between Park Lake Drive and Stewart is unique because all the properties on one side of the street are buffered by a city wash out in the form of a limestone creek that runs through them. Because of this topographical occurrence, there is no 28th or 29th Street and all those 27th Street addresses share a back fence line with 30th Street property owners. We turned on the street and toured what we later would call the "lottery house." The early 50's build was owned by a family who actually won a lottery and installed a bonus room on the back of the house, vinyl siding on the front of the house, and a tall iron fence with electric gates. The real value to this property was the large live oaks that I noticed on the tour after walking into the backyard and seeing my Mandi literally hugging one of them. I can remember trying my hardest to make the calculations in my mind to make purchasing the weird house work as we climbed back into the Suburban and drove the rest of the way down the street.

And then we saw it.

Ten houses down from the lottery house, on the same side of the street, we were stopped in our tracks by a FOR SALE sign jutting from the shaded yard of a little red brick house canopied by live oaks and tall elms. Mandi and I had gotten to the point in our search where we knew there was no time to wait. I quickly parked on the curb and was taking the number of the realtor down when we saw a man come out of the house and walk down the sidewalk. Instinctively and without shame, I jumped out of our Suburban and engaged with the homeowner. He told me he had just placed the sign in the yard fifteen minutes before and the house was open to view by appointment. I told him that our realtor would be by the next day to tour the property. As we turned off 27th we noticed a rainbow had formed in the sky over the trees.

It hasn't been all rainbows and butterfly kisses in our little brick house on 27th St (even though there's been a lot of that.) We've had our fair share of "opportunities" (as a previous mentor, Terry Nelson, would say) even in the six years that we've lived there. One cold morning I happened to see smoke wafting from a roof vent because a previous homeowner had installed an outlet using what looked like a thin speaker wire for the connection. The fire personnel down the street were gracious enough to let me take the ceiling fan down and lay a tarp over Birdie's bed before spraying a conservative amount of water at the small hole in the ceiling that registered some smoldering heat. We also discovered that all the seventy-year-old cast iron plumbing under the house had split open and instead of draining properly had turned into a perforated septic system just beneath the soil line.

Old houses come with their challenges, but just like old cars, that's where their souls are found. They both require that their owners maintain an ongoing relationship with them. There were several times that one of my trucks was letting me know a vacuum plug had fallen off because it sounded slightly different than what I was used to hearing at idle. As so much of this book is about realizing that all things are connected, that's why it's important to know how a few things work in our lives so we can be a part of the restoration process. How else are we going to get the chance to stand there in the driveway wiping our brow with a hand holding a cold one while Jeff from next door says, "Dang, man, that's some good work right there."

Brick By Brick

We added about 600 square feet to our little two-bedroom, two bath house after living there for a couple of years. We put on a new roof at the same time and our first Covid project was priming and painting the old brick and new hardiplank walls. Once we realized we could get a start on project-based mentoring in Waco in our backyard, my good friend, Ralph Bennett led a crew from FBC Malakoff and helped us build a 24x16 ft shop on our property. It now sits next to our mini-ramp and has become a much-needed asset for the ministry and our family.

We get lots of shade over our entire property. We bought the one-and-a-half-acre lot not for the house but for the trees. The front yard near our front porch has always struggled to keep grass. It exists as a dirt patch in the dry season and a mud patch after a rain. So, Mandi and I bought two large pallets of grey brick pavers from the Habitat for Humanity resale store and I got to work setting the metal guide rails, scraping up six inches of topsoil, replacing it with coarse underlay, and tamping down sand on top of that. The delivery truck dropped off pallets in the driveway behind the gate, so I had to carry each brick over to the front yard and then move them again when it was time to put each one in place. The last step was filling the gaps with sand, or in our case, a material which acted more like grout for the pavers.

What only took a paragraph to describe was one of the most substantial house projects I've done after turning forty. I was wiped out after that one. Throughout the course of the project, I considered trying some time-saving techniques and wondered if I really needed to use as much material. I had this inner dialogue with myself because I was either feeling the burden of work and expense in the moment or was trying to forecast the toll it may take in the future.

These are some of the places our minds go when we're confronted with hard work.

How can this be easier? What steps can be omitted? What corners can be cut?

Like all home projects, the brick path leading to the driveway gets used daily. In fact, I start every morning by opening the front blinds and standing at our picture window with one hand in my waist band and the other holding my coffee with my best Ron Swanson expression as I admire the rock-solid gray path. I also watch to see how many neighbors who stop to let their dog relieve itself on our grass quickly jerk on the leash once they make eye contact with me through the steam rising from my cup.

Hard Work's Reward is More Hard Work

Somewhere along the way, "work" turned into a four-letter word. Instead of being blessed by the work of our hands, we started to resent it and tried removing it at all costs. Some folks spend the first two-thirds of their lives working as little as possible and then dream about spending the last third not working at all.

When Lawrence from the film, *Office Space*, asks Peter what he would do with a million dollars, instead of sharing some kind of wild adventure, he dreams about doing "nothing, nothing at all." To which Lawrence replies, "Well, you don't need a million dollars to do nothing, man. Take a look at my cousin: he's broke, don't do s***." BTW, *Office Space* gives an irreverent yet very accurate glimpse of corporate America during the tech boom of the mid to late nineties and I'm sure some of the stereotypes presented still ring true today. It should be noted also that at the end of the movie, Peter finds purpose in the honest and gratifying work of construction.

Just as no person is more valuable than another, no kind of work is more important or more virtuous than another, after all, we are many members of one Body. I've heard friends who value the Gospel greatly say things like "if only (insert a musician or professional athlete name here) would become a Christian, they would do wonders for the Kingdom." While I understand that the name of Jesus would get mentioned more often by these people who have large stages and popular IG accounts, I think we do ourselves a great disservice in equating ministry success by how many social media followers we have. Who is doing the Lord's work in a way that endures, the mainstream musician who releases a Jesus record or the unknown mother who makes parenting decisions based on her core values as they are presented in Scripture? Something to think about.

At the end of the day, every time we yearn for another celebrity to pick up the cross of Christ are we doing so out of the pure hope that even more people will come to know the peace of Jesus, or are we attempting to validate our own credibility in a mainstream society in hopes it will accept us as a Christ follower? Some might want to consider the answer honestly and remember there was a time when a crowd needed to hear Jesus tell them that if they really wanted to connect with God in prayer they need to quit making it a social event and instead go away into their room and do so in quiet.

Jesus spent ample time talking about the virtues of hard work, putting forth our best effort on the daily in all things, and preparing well for the tasks at hand. Matthew 25 begins with the comparison of five wise virgins (band name, I called it) and five foolish ones who paid no attention to the fuel gauge.

He goes next into a story about three servants who were given varying amounts of gold by their master. After some time, two servants had been wise. They invested their amount and saw increase on their investment. The third guy was inhibited by fear. So, he buried his allotment and gained nothing. While the fearful servant missed out on blessings, the two good and faithful servants were free to share in their master's happiness. But they got something else as well. Because they were faithful through their work in a small way, they were now ready to take on even greater responsibility since they had proven trustworthy.

What's hard work's best reward? More hard work.

We exercise this reality in the temporal sense every time we recommend our AC guy to a friend because he does good work. When working with young people through project-based mentoring, we share this spiritual truth that contains a lot of practical application. Want to grow your small business or entrepreneurial venture? Do good work. Want to stand out as a student? Consistently turn in your assignments. Want to carry yourself with an uncommon integrity in relationships? Say what you mean and mean what you say.

We are entering into a time in history when being the kind of worker who simply does her best and does what she says she's going do without an excuse for why she couldn't will no longer be the standard but instead she will perform head and shoulders over her colleagues. The standard for what is acceptable in work is steadily dropping each year.

My eldest daughter recently took a college-freshman-level quiz which featured objective multiple-choice questions followed by a subcategory of questions in which the test taker was to rate her confidence level of each answer. We live in a time when there needs to be a value for not just what the right answer is but also how the test taker FELT about giving each answer? I'll let you draw your own conclusions about what this means to objective truth and letting our "yes be yes and our no be no." Matt 5:37

Speaking of college, we're not all academic wunderkinds. I made all the Bs in high school with never doing homework and carried that philosophy through my undergrad since I always took a full schedule of courses on Tues/Thurs and worked with Cody and John the bodybuilder doing property management (aka mowing) Mon/Wed/Fri to pay for that degree. Here are the two secrets to my success as an undergrad:

1) Go to class. Every day. Don't miss a day. Ever. Don't feel like going to class? Ok, I'm so sorry. Please go to class. Feeling a lil sicky? Ugh. Hate it for you. Go to class. Being there daily meant I never had to play catch up. It also meant that if I was struggling with my final grade as we ended the semester, my professor would see I was one of the few students who showed up every day and that allowed me some leverage. Speaking of professors...

2) Know your professor and make sure she knows you. Small class sizes make this easy. During the first week of school, introduce yourself to all your profs at the end of class. Tell them you appreciate their investment and look forward to the semester. If you struggle with an assignment, make an appointment during your instructor's office hours, ask your questions, and resolve the issues. You can do this whether you're one of fifteen students or 150.

These two basic priorities paved the way for what I consider a successful undergraduate career. It yielded experience and knowledge in communicating with academic leaders and, on two occasions, improved my final grade by a letter, not by my request, but because my instructors valued initiative and hard work.

Work as Worship

Once Adam breathed his first breath, he got up and put his work boots on. The first recorded occupation on earth was that of farmer (Gen 2:15) and animal-namer (Gen 2:18-20). He was given these responsibilities even before given a partner. This shows us two things: one, that work is a blessing and two, we were created for community. While you can read more about the harmful effects of sin in Genesis 3, we can't deny work was designed as a blessing before it was a burden.

For those who can value it in its various forms, work can be thought of as worship. If our jobs are what we spend the most of our waking hours doing, why not redeem them knowing that what we're doing goes well beyond what is seen. Many folks wake up each day feeling their cross is overwhelming, unsustainable, or doesn't amount to enough in the greater picture of eternity. But when purpose follows identity as naturally as when David recognized Mephibosheth for who he was and then reinstated his authority over land and resources, he showed us the needed connection between identity and purpose.

Sometimes our crosses feel like they are more than we can bear.

By design, they are.

The burden was never meant to be ours alone.

*So, what ever happened to the $80,000 check that was meant as seed money for taking Middleman on as a full-time endeavor? The short answer is that it never happened. We were told the funds would be made available a few short months after we moved to Waco and started working to build the ministry. That process took longer than expected. Once we received the physical check in the mail, we were told to wait for a few weeks to deposit it while some key donors made deposits to the church that would be designated to Middleman. We then were told that two donors pulled out of the agreement so the funds would never be available.

The $80,000 check adventure served us well in two ways. First, without it being promised, I am unsure I would have pulled the trigger on leaving church work and taking Middleman full-time without the financial and emotional buffer the expectation of the funds provided. While I had no idea of how God would sustain us after those funds were depleted, they gave me a confidence of knowing I wasn't moving my family away from steady income and insurance to start at zero without backers.

We were also well-served when the funds never materialized as I believe the financial padding would have created a false sense of security and may have slowed my intentionality in creating programming, serving others, and connecting with community members. Over the first year of moving my family (and Middleman) to Waco, my confidence in the Lord's will, promise, and providence reached new levels. I always tell people that we will continue to give away skateboards and Bibles for as long as we have them on hand and for over ten years now, we have done just that without ever running out of either of them.

My hope in sharing this story is to remind you that if God is calling you to exercise your faith in a way that scares you tremendously, you need not fear for if or how He will carry out His work in your life. In the case of the promised funds, there were momentary hurt feelings and fear, but no permanent damage to my friendship with Michael. He has proven himself as a generous supporter of Middleman over the years and remains one of my best friends.

CHAPTER 8

CRAZY TRAIN

(Community is Where Purpose Gets Perfected)

Crazy, but that's how it goes
Millions of people living as foes
Maybe it's not too late
To learn how to love
And forget how to hate
-from Ozzy Osborne's "Crazy Train"

The Hick from French Lick

Do you read biographies? I'm not sure why I've always been as interested in them as I have. I don't care for celebrity-ism. I realize it's one of our nation's GNPs. It's always struck me as odd that meeting or being near a person who has been featured in some sort of media creates a chemical reaction in our bodies that makes us want to stumble through a brief conversation with the person or have them give us something with their signature on it.

This observation isn't from witnessing it from other people. I'm very guilty of it myself even though I haven't met any popularly famous folks. Ron Swanson's reaction to seeing a builder at the Indiana Fine Woodworking Association Award has been more my speed: "Mary mother of God. That's Christian Becksvoort! He's the modern master of the shaker style. I never dreamed that I would see him in the flesh."

I've had similar experiences meeting skaters who I grew up idolizing and regional musicians who made a profound impression on me as a young adult. I once engaged Jimmie Vaughan in the frozen section of HEB and made small talk as he stood slowly drumming a set of plastic coat hangers on the outside of his knee while talking about how, yes, he likes living in Austin very much, thank you. And yeah, he looked like he had just walked off stage dressed in all black with Ray Bans on. (Work some JV tunes like "Don't Cha Know" or "In the Middle of the Night" into your playlist and then listen to some Buddy Guy.)

Fun fact: The first autobiography I can remember reading was, "Drive: The Story of My Life" by Larry Bird.

Fun fact II (The Return of the Fun Fact): The first thing that I downloaded and printed out from the brand-new thing called the world wide web was a photograph of Larry Bird. I don't know why he was the subject of my search, save, and print journey. I have no other Larry Bird stories and I am sorry about that.

Biographies give us a chance to hear the broader story of those we believe have a story worth knowing. Since reading about #33 as a teenager, I have read biographies over several presidents, actors, military leaders, other athletes, artists, innovative businesspeople, musicians, historical figures, and professional skateboarders (ok only Christian Hosoi and Tony Hawk but that's still plural). There are common threads that run through all noteworthy stories. First, everyone's life is marked by struggle and loss. Second, everyone endures hardships and learns valuable lessons they channel into their ultimate success.

Another truth about people whose stories we care about is that no one does it all on their own.

Self-Made Men (and Women) Do Not Exist

There is simply no such thing as a self-made man.

Do titans of industry defy the odds to work their way up the corporate ladder? Yes. Do some of our greatest athletes of all time overcome systemic racism or abusive family lives? They do. But as we begin to consider how community is the daily practice of purpose, it's essential to understand what role other people play in our development and what role we will play in theirs.

Everyone's first day on the job begins with a cruise down a dark tunnel toward the light. While our ties to Mama are cut within moments, we still need to be cared for immediately by adults in every way possible after birth or we won't survive a day.

For some reason, my social media feed insists that I am interested in or that I need to watch clips of professional MMA fighters hitting each other. This is a common video theme that presents itself in my scroll. I believe my phone's listening to me think about, talk about, and watch the films Rocky-Rocky V, Rocky Balboa, Creed, and Creed II is probably to blame for this. As much as I do appreciate traditional boxing, the sheer brutality of MMA and similar modern fighting sport is hard for me to stomach. But from what little I have seen, it's clear that some of those men and women who enter the octagon are as tough as a human being can be.

But even Frankie Edgar and Diego Sanchez needed people to nurture them into not only becoming weapons of mass destruction but growing as children, developing through their teenage years, and learning what it means to operate as functioning adults.

Anyone who has done anything, whether great or small, in this life was able to because someone else offered him enough healthy community to make it a reality. Watch any of the inspirational biopics that showcase athletes and musicians, (*The Buddy Holly Story, Remember the Titans, Ray, Invincible, Talladega Nights*) and you'll see time and again that our heroes were right on the edge of ultimate discouragement and failure before being given just one more shot to prove they had what it takes to overcome obstacles and succeed.

When Johnny Cash went into Sun Records with an unconvincing gospel song in the film, *Walk the Line*, the man at the soundboard, Sam Phillips, gives a monologue about digging deeper:

"If you was hit by a truck and you was lying out there in that gutter dying, and you had time to sing one song. Huh? One song that people would remember before you're dirt. One song that would let God know how you felt about your time here on Earth. One song that would sum you up. You tellin' me that's the song you'd sing? That same Jimmy Davis tune we hear on the radio all day, about your peace within, and how it's real, and how you're gonna shout it? Or... would you sing somethin' different. Somethin' real. Somethin' you felt. Cause I'm telling you right now, that's the kind of song people want to hear. That's the kind of song that truly saves people."

Cash then sings "Folsom Prison Blues" and that's...the rest of the story.

Christians are Weird

The apostle Peter wrote a letter to young Christians who

were enduring active persecution throughout five regions of Asia Minor. As an encouragement for his friends to hold fast during that difficult time he tells them to "be ready to give an answer for the hope that you profess but do it with gentleness and respect."

There are many reasons to love this instruction and see it as one that connected people should emulate in their daily life. Peter's request is that Christians would first be doing things that create a response. In essence, he is saying that when people ask what our deal is, you are prepared to answer with a profession of hope. We reveal ourselves to be a people connected to God AND the questioner as we prioritize gentleness and respect within our friendship to them.

Oh man, the art of explanation.

Would you agree that our actions go much further to reinforce our beliefs than our beliefs determine our actions? Isn't that the definition of faith we see in Hebrews? A surety of what isn't there and a certainty of what we're blind to.

Our churches are littered with habitually bored attenders who have worn a rut into their pews and a desensitized glaze over their hearts. But we're all built for a fight so instead of doing the hard work of loving the least of these, they fire their shots through strongly voiced emails to the pastor and worship leader in their plight to have new and interesting methods of communication from the pulpit on a weekly basis. They think the problem in the church has more to do with song selection, volume settings, and a preacher's illustrations and less to do with their own ability to remember their own faces after walking away from the mirror (James 1:22-23). There is often more energy spent armchair quarterbacking over Sunday lunch at Luby's than service and sacrificial living from Monday to Saturday.

For many who doubt their faith or wonder if God is still for them, they don't have to look far to understand it's not that following Christ is too complex. On the contrary, it's too brutally simple. After all, what does the Lord ask but that you act justly, love mercy, and walk humbly with Him? (Micah 6:8) That's it. Just as Saul struggled to understand that obedience was more important than unsolicited sacrifice, we see the prophet Micah, in 700 BC, addressing the same condition of the human heart which so often yields itself within the vast complications of trying to figure out what in the world God could be thinking so far away, up there in Heaven.

The worshipper is befuddled with doubt and overwhelming fear when considering what will please a perfect God:

With what shall I come before the Lord
and bow down before the exalted God?
Shall I come before him with burnt offerings,
with calves a year old?
Will the Lord be pleased with thousands of rams,
with ten thousand rivers of olive oil?
Shall I offer my firstborn for my transgression,
the fruit of my body for the sin of my soul?
-Micah 6:6-7

Holy cow, what will please God? Let me list sacrifices and resources too great for me to ever bear. Let me make this harder than it has to be since it is the great and mysterious God of Abraham that we're talking about. Surely, He asks more than I can imagine and requires more than I can give.

But, He provides the answer to our questions in three simple acts within six words. Three verbs. Two adverbs. One noun.

He has shown you, O mortal, what is good.
And what does the Lord require of you?
To ***act justly*** *and to* ***love mercy***
and to ***walk humbly*** *with your God. -Micah 6:8*

Act Justly

It begins with a verb: Act. Do. Live your life even before you have it all figured out. Because if you wait to have all the answers, you never will have time left to "act" on anything. But how are we to act? Justly. Righteously. In other words, walk with integrity in your steps. Carry yourself as one who prioritizes justice.

Before we started having kids, we had a Bulldog named Zoe. Owning a Bulldog is like owning an Italian sportscar. You are the belle of the ball on walks around the neighborhood and you make fast friends at the coffee shop. But it comes at a great price in initial cost and maintenance. Once I learned that dog dermatologists exist and that our dog would benefit from one's service, I called it quits on expensive niche animals (I feel the same way about Italian sports cars too).

One day while taking Zoe to the normal vet, I returned to my 1999 Saturn to find it missing from the parking space where I left it. My confusion was quickly abated when I looked over to see my car forty feet away resting against a parked Toyota. In my haste to get my dog out of the car and on her leash without her running off, I forgot to put my manual transmission in gear and set the parking brake. So, while Zoe and I were in the doctor's office, my car slowly rolled down the parking lot and into an unsuspecting parked Camry.

I confess my knee-jerk response was to note that no one

noticed the damage to the other car. There was a time as a young driver that I would have been tempted to get in my car and drive away. As inconvenient as it was, I entered each of the small businesses in the strip center to find the owner of the damaged vehicle and share my insurance information with her.

Every day we get multiple chances to respond to things and be proactive in ways that reflect our value for acting justly. When the opportunity to do the right thing presents itself, we should do it without hesitation and before we give ourselves a chance to talk ourselves out of it. When you see a wrong, address it, and work to right it. When you see someone in need, stop to help. Act justly.

Love Mercy

Acting justly means doing the hard work of making decisions that benefit others around us. It is empowered greatly when we consider what it means to love mercy. We are commanded to practice a verb: love. The act of loving means we sacrifice ourselves for the sake of someone or something else. In this case, it's mercy. If a working definition of grace is to receive a good gift we don't deserve, we can understand mercy to reside on the other end of the spectrum in that we aren't burdened by something unwanted we rightfully had coming to us based on our words or actions. To show mercy to someone is to hold back judgement or punishment when it would have been fitting to "give them what they deserve."

Showing mercy is one of the most difficult things a person can do. It's hard because our brains are programmed for balance, resolution, and justifiable cause and effect. When you break a law, you owe something to society for your infraction. Even in personal relationships, we are excellent at keeping score and making sure the scales of justice are held evenly.

Micah 6 goes beyond instructing us to recognize mercy as we interact with creation. We're told to love it. Sacrifice for it. Be consumed by it. Let it be our muse and our joy. Let us look for unconventional ways we can show mercy to those around us and those far off from us. Imagine having a mindset so locked in to giving people an undeserved break that we would sing "Come Thou fount of every blessing. Tune my heart to sing Thy grace. **Streams of mercy never ceasing.** Call for songs of loudest praise" and mean it.

This is a work only God can do in us and through us. Showing mercy is an act reserved for Heaven because it's allowing people to take advantage of you. There is an incredible amount of "injustice" within mercy. I can easily think of twenty people I know who don't deserve my recognizing them as friends because of what they have done or said to or about me or someone I love. And how I consider them is the most direct way I can gauge my love for mercy. What if, as Ozzy states, "it's not too late to learn how to love and forget how to hate"?

Walk Humbly

And we're back to the verb and adverb. But we're not just told to move with pious self-denial here. Because even in that there is far too much room for interpretation and faulty judgment. Where do we walk? When do we walk? What do we take with us?

The most important truth we can know about the HOW of acting justly and loving mercy is found in the third part of

Micah 6:8 which tells us that we are to walk humbly with our God. Jesus says "follow me" thirteen times in the Gospels. There are nearly 60 times throughout scripture that mention following God. It reminds us of Luke 9:23 which tells us to deny ourselves, take up our cross, and then we're ready to follow. There is no room to do our thing AND God's. You can't serve two masters. Following God means understanding daily that He knows what's best for you and is willing and able to lead you when you make the decision to follow Him.

But just as I can explain blues music to you by showing you how the notes of E, A, and B relate to each other in the 12-bar system, you can spend the rest of your life studying the greatest blues musicians of all time and still never come close to mastering it. You can agree that acting justly, loving mercy, and walking humbly with God is the way to go but it doesn't mean you'll practice those six words.

The biggest problem with the disconnect from the head to the hands is that it's so easy to "believe" something yet never apply it. Peter's instruction is incredible because it leads with the presumption that you and I as Christ followers are living so obediently that our "evangelism" would look less like mustering up the courage to ask somebody on the street if they will go to heaven if they die tonight and more like being in a place to take the time and effort to explain to someone who doesn't yet know Christ why in the world you act the way you do.

Why do you react the way you do in the face of adversity?

Why are you peaceful when everybody else in the office was so offended by a thing?

Why did you stand up for that person when no one else did?

There's a chasm between "believing" and doing these days. We can amen everything the pastor says yet when it comes down to it, are we any different than those outside the church (aside from our dutiful Sunday morning church attendance)?

Where does Christ shine the brightest in our lives? Is it our involvement in our church? Is it in our championing excellent moral living which includes never cussing or drinking when other church folks are around? Are we at our best when we say Jesus above all, so we have no interest in things like civil rights and environmentalism because those are political issues?

What if we could profess the hope we have in Jesus through these avenues?

Peter would encourage us to be all about Jesus all the time. He links this to being our source of hope, after all. But then he says that we should also be prepared to explain within the context of gentleness and respect. This is less of a "we love Jesus, yes we do" pep rally and more of a know-your-audience kind of cadence that allows us as the hope bearers to stop thinking about evangelism as a marketing strategy and instead consider someone who has yet to know Christ as Jesus himself sees her.

To explain our actions in gentleness involves self-awareness and seeks to communicate and represent Christ rightly. Jesus called himself gentle and humble in heart. He knew that throughout every generation there would be weary souls who were tired and unable to bear the load of life, no matter how put together they look in public. Jesus knows that the burdened and tired find a rest in Him that cannot be found anywhere else. He said that His yoke is easy, and His burden is light. (Matthew 11:28-30. More on this in chapter 11.) A little compassion goes a long way. If the heart stance for the average Christian would be one of humility and gentleness coupled with an intentionality of sharing this hope that we profess with others, the world might look a little more like heaven.

Peter says our evangelism should be one part gentleness and another part respect. Think about how counterintuitive that is when you share Jesus with someone. How often has it been that you share your faith with a person out of your respect for them? This you-before-me kind of ideology should empower our application of the Gospel at every turn.

This passage was Peter Frampton (it came alive!) when visiting Gallup, NM a few years ago. My good friend Cory and I drove from Lubbock across the state to check in on his friend, Pastor Aaron, and family. While spending a few days in Gallup, we decided to visit the public skate park on the Rez. I was apprehensive from the beginning. Something to be aware of about skateboarding culture is that spots and parks will often have a set group of locals who protect their sovereignty and will reject visitors quickly. I've never seen this play out more clearly than when visiting the famous Venice Beach skate park that I had only grown up seeing in magazines, skate videos, and even I the 80s skate movie *Thrashin'*. I not only saw local skaters firsthand telling visiting skaters to leave, but they also went so far as to throw their boards down into the bowl at those dudes letting them know they weren't welcome. "Beat it, ya Vall jerk!"

When Cory and I pulled up to the skate park in Gallup, it seemed chill. There were a few skaters riding while others were kicking back on some ledges and walls talking.

The power of skateboarding is and always has been unique. When I ride a skateboard, I don't stop being an old guy in his late forties, however, simultaneously I'm taken back to how it felt over thirty-five years ago when I started. My heart still races every time I skate but especially so when pulling up to a new spot. On that day in Gallup, all senses were fired up. I was cruising around the park, making sure everybody was cool, and listening for anybody yelling at me and any boards coming in as missiles to take me out. A few minutes in, I realized I wasn't getting mad dogged by anybody, and I could skate up to some locals and say what's up. One of the first skaters I met was Jeremy Todacheenie. He and his wife own the skate shop that sits next to the park. They are both good skaters who love their scene and started their shop out of their living room before renting a legit spot nearby.

It didn't take long before Jeremy asked about where I'm from and why I was in town. The next topic of conversation as we stood talking was my board. That day I was riding one of our Giving Tree decks and had the chance to tell Jeremy what Middleman is all about and why we put the well-known graphic on our boards. It was an incredible honor to tell him about Jesus' love that is sacrificial and perfect. The exchange I had with Jeremy led to our inviting him and his wife to dinner later that evening and a few months after that trip, we partnered with their shop to hold a free skate camp and competition using shop riders at the park for the community.

That type of event is a far-cry from a conversation I had one day with a non-skater college student who was asking my advice about ministering at the public skate park in her community. Her idea was to get other college students and some volunteers from her church to spend a day out at the park playing worship music, feeding skaters, and having someone preach over a loudspeaker to the skaters while they ate. She said that her crew could all wear t-shirts that said "OCCUPY THE SKATEPARK" because they were claiming that place for Jesus... (cue the record scratch sound effect).

I hope at this point you see the difference between these two approaches. I believe God can use anybody for His glory. But sharing hope out of gentleness and respect can be effective without OCCUPY-themed clothing. Here are three professions that speak into how we can practice our purpose in community:

The Three Hats of the Mentor

Among a plethora of other job titles, parents, mentors, and teachers can be framed as farmers, miners, and tour guides. These three professions give us an accurate framework for how to understand this noble work and how we can best relate to our kids and mentees.

The Farmer

There was a time when people grew the food we eat on farms. These people would prepare soil, plant seed, maintain the crop for a season, and then reap what was sown. There are still folks making food this way, but they wear Chacos and sell tomatoes under canopies for three dollars each in parking lots on Saturday mornings.

The traditional farmer is a great metaphor because investing in people is farming. It is day to day. It is a slow and unsexy process. A friend who runs a skate ministry in Indiana said once that he "moves at the speed of relationship" which reinforces the idea of slow and steady. It relies on time-tested principles.

Just like farming, you can do all the right things within your parenting and mentoring relationships, but it won't guarantee expectations will be met. Farmers expect the unexpected knowing that there are variables like pests and weather conditions that exist beyond their control that affect a healthy crop. Parents and mentors who realize and value the sovereignty of God have the benefit of knowing that, while their leadership is integral to the process of health and growth, their kids and mentees ultimately belong to God. This should breed a confidence in the hearts of these "investors" knowing that the burden doesn't totally land on them.

Like a farmer whose role has become obsolete by a society that has prioritized progress through technology worship, today's parents and mentors can find much of their work centering on addressing some of the havoc that technology and a breakdown of genuine relationship has wreaked on young hearts and minds.

The Miner

Like the farmer, the work of the miner is daily and goes on with little to no fanfare. Miners are unique in that they don't bring value into an environment, they instead uncover what is already there, in the dark and under the rubble. If you grew up going on summer mission trips as a teenager, it was there you probably learned the valuable difference between those who mistakenly believe they are "taking Jesus into" a situation and instead that missionaries are visitors who enjoy the honor of watching God work where He was before they ever got there. He will also be at work there long after the visitors leave.

Mining within parenting and mentoring means drawing

out from our kids what we know to be the best of them and what they need to see as well. This is no simple task. It takes discernment and patience. It requires control when things are loud and confidence when things are silent. The miner has the vision to see value where few others can.

The Tour Guide

The first quality of a good tour guide is they must physically be in the environment they are attempting to showcase. I once read the work of the mentor is to show up, live out, and speak in. There just isn't any substitute for being there. Some of the best tour guides in existence are those who truly love where they work. They research the history of their environment. They know things that others don't. They relate to visitors in such a way so they can discover for themselves what is exceptional about the place they are in. Parents and mentors should see beauty and value everywhere and help guide their kids to discover the same.

Farmers farm, miners mine, tour guides guide, and, as Little Marie reminds Rocky when he's struggling to figure out how to address the fire in the basement, "fighters fight." We must remember to keep working on our craft as investors in young people.

David was so confident in his own purpose that he was free to offer the same to Mephibosheth and help him make the connection between who he was and what he needed to do. That was essential for Mephibosheth and it's essential for our children, students, and those we mentor today.

CHAPTER 9

WE BELONG

(We are Created for Community)

We belong to the light, we belong to the thunder
We belong to the sound of the words
we've both fallen under
Whatever we deny or embrace for worse or for better
We belong, we belong, we belong together
-from Pat Benatar's "We Belong"

There was a time during the 80s when it got popular to produce mainstream songs with heavenly themes. Bryan Adams was finding it hard to believe that y'all were in heaven with you lying there in his arms. A few years later Belinda Carlisle knew that in heaven, loves comes first so she was committing to make heaven a place on earth. After the tragic death of his young son, Eric Clapton co-wrote and recorded "Tears in Heaven" in which he sang about being strong and carrying on, as he knows he doesn't belong, here in heaven.

The concept of heaven on earth predates 80s and early 90s pop songs. On one occasion after they hear him pray, Jesus' closest friends ask if He will teach them how to pray.

So, He does:

"Our Father in heaven,
hallowed be your name,

your kingdom come,
your will be done,
on earth as it is in heaven.
Give us today our daily bread.
And forgive us our trespasses,
as we also have forgiven those who trespass against us.
And lead us not into temptation,
but deliver us from evil.
For yours is the Kingdom and the power and the glory forever.
Amen."

Author Brennan Manning said he begins each day by reciting the Lord's Prayer before his feet hit the floor. The progression and intentionality of the model prayer gives us an excellent framework and justification for mimicking Manning's daily routine.

Our father in heaven,

To begin each day with the first words out of our mouths speaking to God and our identity is noteworthy. By calling out to our Father, we immediately see ourselves as His sons and daughters. We recognize God in heaven as reigning in perfection like no one and nothing else we can imagine.

Hallowed be Your Name

Recognizing God's name is holy. It is set apart and true, perfectly distinguished from all other names.

Your Kingdom come,
Your will be done,
On earth as it is in heaven

Living as a person of hope means trusting God and desiring with all that we are that He is near. We welcome God's presence and with it His will. His purpose is meant to be our purpose. It's a funny thing to pray that the Lord would do a work somewhere out there in the world without wondering what part we need to play directly in it. When Jesus makes his famous "the harvest is plentiful, but the workers are few" speech, he goes onto tell his closest friends that they need to pray to the Lord of the harvest for workers. What does Jesus then do immediately in the next chapter? He sends those same guys out in the field to freely give! It's as if Jesus was telling the disciples that once they start praying for God's will to be done, they would discover that they themselves would be called on to serve.

Before we move on, spend another beat thinking about it--something being on earth (here) as it is in heaven (there). Maybe this is where some of that imagination can step in and show us a glimpse of the potential future. I know we don't have a clear and definitive understanding of what (or even when) heaven is. I grew up watching movies like *Heaven Can Wait* and *Oh God!* From the late 70s that gave us Hollywood's take on God and heaven. The recent show *The Good Place* offered a hot take on the place of heaven, death, and good vs evil but sidestepped the presence of a Creator for the creative adventures of the created. But I think we can agree that heaven is good. It is optimal, even. Calling on God's will to realize the place and power of heaven in our small lives on a Tuesday morning is a good thing.

Consider your kids for a moment. What would you imagine for them if things in their life right now could be heaven on earth? What kind of character traits would you dream for them to possess as young adults? How would you imagine their lives to look like in the family they will help build some day, in their careers, and in their community? Spending some time considering these things can help to guide your prayer life for them and your parenting or mentoring style.

Give us today our daily bread

The request harkens back to the ancient Israelite captives who were set free by God's power from the Egyptians. In the book of Exodus, you can read about God providing for His people in the form of manna, which was described as a thin, flaky food that would appear each morning on the ground and that the Israelites could take and eat. Because of the sabbath, the people were to gather enough manna for two days but every other day of the week they were to gather only what they needed that day. If, for fear of their not being enough, people gathered more than the day's allotment, they would discover the manna to be maggot-infested and unable to eat. This is a metaphor for us today because we know God's mercies are new every morning and the communion we enjoy with Him is meant for daily consumption.

This section also identifies we are aware that everything we have comes from God. As the old saying goes, "the harder I work, the luckier I get." That stance, if taken to the extreme breeds prideful ignorance but while recognizing God's provision, we are reminded of our place of responsibility in it.

And forgive us our trespasses,
as we also have forgiven those who trespass against us.

Every Sunday morning when I am led through this prayer in our church service, I appreciate this section as the first line is preempted in practice by the second line but there is the implication that stands as a litmus test for all who say it. We're asking God to forgive our failures against Him and others while recognizing that we have forgiven others of theirs. What a great place to work from.

And lead us not into temptation,
but deliver us from evil.
For Yours is the Kingdom and the power and the glory forever.
Amen

God is our help, our Deliverer. We recognize His presence by being mindful of His Kingdom, His ability when considering His power, and His substance when marveling at His glory. Whenever anyone says "amen" after a prayer, they are using shorthand to say, "so be it" or "may it be so."

The Tale of Two Communities (Convenient Community vs True Community)

In his book, *The Shaping of Things to Come*, Michael Frost presents the reader with two opposing philosophies for achieving and maintaining community. In the "Centered Set" people are attracted to one another through a Christ-centric community based on the sharing of truth and display of conviction through service. Think about when Jesus would insert himself in social situations, heal those who needed it, and share truth or teach a lesson. This is also known as the "well approach" as it gives us the mental image of a water well dug in the middle of a town or pasture where people or animals can come and have their thirst quenched. There is always equal access in this approach. The progression of this type of community would begin with belonging, go then to influencing social behavior, and finally land on working to form our belief system. (Belong->Behave->Believe)

Frost's "Bounded Set" focuses on forming and keeping community defined within a parameter or fenced area. This highly defined (and often defended) series of connected walls clearly determines who is "in" and who is "out." The traditional bounded, or fence/gate, structure to community includes the first step of believing. What do you believe to be true? Do your beliefs line up well enough with my beliefs to allow you entrance into my community? The next stop on this community train is behavior. Are you doing the acceptable things based on what you claim to believe? When these two areas are deemed moral or appropriate enough, then, and only then, are you given the chance to truly belong. (Believe->Behave->Belong)

You can draw your own conclusions about the highwall style of community building. It is the process most employed by communities everywhere. As much as I hate to admit it, it is also the primary process for many church communities. And why wouldn't it be? It is simple and direct. Good fences, after all, make good neighbors.

It is also very clean and convenient. Things are black or white. You're in or you're out. Unfortunately, it does not make for deep and lasting community because it is performance based. And people, by their nature, even those who have been redeemed, if given enough time, will fail and disappoint you.

There are two ways to live your life and process community, you can build those walls and do your best to keep them fortified and sanitized, or you can radiate hospitality in all its messiness and tension.

Jairo

The first thing I noticed when I rolled up to the skate park was his board. It was an early-80s Galaxy Skateboard made in Dallas. Those boards were unique in that instead of being made from seven-ply maple, they were constructed out of a sheet of composite plastic attached to a thin sheet of aluminum that the bottom graphics were applied to. The eighth-grader's Galaxy had seen better days as the plastic was badly dried out and had cracked in several places making it almost impossible to ride. The thin piece of aluminum was all that was keeping the deck together.

I hadn't introduced myself to him yet, but I enjoyed watching how the injured skateboard didn't keep Jairo from trying rock and rolls in the small bowl at the park. It reminded me of being in junior high and learning tricks on a board that is working against you every step of the way from a worn off tail or rusty bearings.

By the end of the day, I had skated with Jairo, shown him some tricks to try out, and asked if his skateboard was special to him. He told me it was just an old board and the only one he had access to. I left the park telling him that I would bring him a new set up the next day but that he'd have to trade me his old Galaxy for the new Middleman.

The next day as I pulled up to the park, I saw him riding his old board on the street course. He was more than happy to hand it over to me as I gave him a Middleman and shared the graphic's meaning with him.

Over the next few years, I got to watch Jairo get better at skating as he put in hours at the park and grew stronger through high school. I enjoyed giving him more skate equipment and hired him to work on our project vehicles in the garage. He hit a rough patch in his junior year and decided to leave high school to start working. Once we started offering more local skate camps in Waco, we made it a point to get Jairo involved as an instructor as it gave him purpose and gave us a chance to pay him as he was supporting himself and his pregnant girlfriend.

Last year it was a joy to work alongside Jairo in several skate camps he helped with after getting off his day job in construction. On the last day of camp, I told him I had a surprise for him. His eyes lit up as I pulled the Galaxy board out of the van and handed it over to him almost five years to the day we first met.

The Bible includes a letter from the Apostle Peter he wrote to the scattered young church. In it, he told them "Above all, love each other deeply, because love covers over a multitude of sins. Offer hospitality to one another without grumbling." 1 Peter 4:8-9

He's telling us to love each other lavishly, with depth and liberality. This love that we can radiate has a power to overwhelm and dissipate sin. Love defeats shortcomings that would otherwise give us self-righteous justification to allow our flesh to feel about someone else who misses the mark often enough for us to open the gate and push them outside the community walls. Peter goes onto say that we extend hospitality to folks. Not mere friendliness and kind words. Hospitality. May our community experience be one where we "house" one another.

Do you have a family member's home that you feel most comfortable in? My wife's birthday is on Christmas Eve (yeah, it's a bummer.) I started dating Mandi when I was 18 and she was 15. I had just graduated high school and she was in the summer before her sophomore year. (Take it easy, we've been together for over 30 years now.) Since getting married in 1999, we have spent most Christmas Eve nights over at my in-law's house. The tradition is now one that my kids love as they get to spend that time with Papa, Mimi, the cousins, and other extended family. While my kids love seeing their other grandparents and family members throughout holidays and other times of the year, Papa's house is special. It's a place they feel welcome and comfortable. Instead of feeling pressured to burn energy to make it through time there, they feel relaxed, restored, and full of pound cake after a visit. That's what hospitality should result in: a restoration and relaxation that charges our batteries. It can be practiced by welcoming family, neighbors, friends, and strangers into our homes.

The Danger of Community?

Most people rely on a community for practical and relational purposes. It's what Martin Luther King spoke of when saying that "We are caught in an inescapable network of mutuality, tied in a single garment of destiny. Whatever affects one directly affects all indirectly." We can't make it alone. We were never meant to. Throughout history, a strong community was needed to keep people alive. That hasn't changed. There is something wonderful about being included with people who share something more substantial than geographical location. Something that, when shared, makes individuals feel less lonely. A community is a safe place. Rex explains in *Napoleon Dynamite* that "At Rex Kwan Do, we use the buddy system. No more flying solo. You need somebody watching your back AT ALL TIMES!" Bow to your sensei.

But there is something potentially dangerous about

communities. A well-defined and invested-in community can be a place of safety and comfort for its members. It can also unknowingly create barriers that work to define who is "in" and who is "out." Group members can forget about the world outside of their community, or regard other communities with subtle prejudices. Things can turn into M. Night Shyamalan's *The Village* quickly. Many small groups within churches can suffer from this especially if they feel they have worked hard to get the chemistry or the temperature of the group just right.

There was an active and friendly family in our youth group some years ago. The parents were Sunday school teachers and their polite kids played instruments and sang in the youth worship band that would lead teenagers on Wednesday nights and Sunday mornings. One of the girls from our youth ministry asked if she could sing with the band and I told her she absolutely could because the group is always open to anyone who wants to join.

I was wrong.

One of the band moms told me the well-defined group of teenagers worked too hard to achieve the specific sound they were after. She was concerned that adding someone with less ability would be a bad fit for the band. The rejected teenage girl was crushed, and as the youth pastor, I was confused. The decision to keep one of the teenagers who attended our youth program from serving and leading in the youth band was unfortunate. It was also the tipping point for the girl who decided to leave our church and find a group who would accept her along with her limited abilities and experience. Ugh.

David knew the power and importance of community as

he offered it to Mephibosheth because if the new land manager was going to get a grasp on his leadership position, it would require David investing time and effort into him. We can all but guarantee that Mephibosheth was going to struggle in his new role. Even though it was rightfully his because he was Jonathan's son, he would be commanding a staff, resources, livestock, and citizens. Did David's rightful appointment of Mephibosheth mean that the people affected would automatically accept him as their leader? We have no record of that either way, but we can imagine the struggled because we know how reluctant to change we are. It surely created some issues. Mephibosheth would need David to equip and encourage him daily and I am sure it wouldn't prove to be the most convenient situation for the man of margin and his new friend who called himself a dead dog. It was not just good for David to provide community to Mephibosheth; it was essential for his success.

CHAPTER 10

STAND LIKE STEEL

(Community is Inconvenient)

You've got to stand,
stand like steel,
Nobody ever promised a garden of roses,
Nobody gets to Heaven without a fight, that's right,
Stand like steel.
-from Randy Stonehill's "Stand Like Steel"

The Cold Chair

Lorene Barnard was born in 1909 somewhere near Wichita Falls, TX. Family folklore has it that she was a student of Georgia O'Keefe's when the famed artist was a gym instructor in Canyon, Texas many years ago. In 1973 I was born to her son, my dad, John, and my mom, Kathy. As I mentioned before, I was raised between two homes as my parents divorced when I was two years old then both remarried and I spent most of my childhood living at the Guevara's house in South Houston and visiting the Barnard's house in the Park Place area of Houston. Nardi lived in a white pier and beam on Weir Drive in the Glenbrook area that her husband

Bill built for her and their three children, Donna, Joel, and my dad, John Mark. I never knew my grandfather as he died when my dad was thirteen years old. He worked in lumber and could bid a job so well he'd only have a foot of 2x4 left over after construction. I now own one thing that belonged to my grandfather: one of his handsaws. I like to think it was one he used for the house on Weir but that may be as true as Georgie O'Keefe leading my grandmother in jumping jacks.

Nardi's house was a peaceful sanctuary for me growing up. (Nardi was named as such because some very young children in her classroom couldn't pronounce "Mrs. Barnard" so she JLoed everybody from that point on and became "Nardi"). Throughout my childhood, visits to her house included endless art projects at the kitchen table, games of "I Spy" in her living room, and humid days in August sitting in the chilly gold chair that sat directly in front of the large window unit used to cool the entire house. Nardi would take me during my young teenage years to Mervyn's for a few Bugle Boy shirts and to Almeda Mall's Visible Changes for a fresh cut.

The best thing Nardi did was pray for me.

It didn't mean as much back then, but I distinctly remember her telling me, almost daily, that she was praying for me. Before I became a Christian, she prayed for my salvation. She prayed for my safety. She prayed for my future. I am certain that her prayers made a difference when it came to the very things that she laid at Jesus' feet on my behalf over the years while I stayed determined to mess things up as much as I could.

James 5:16 tells us to pray for each other so that God will

heal us and that the prayers of a righteous person are powerful and effective. There is amazing power in prayer and all too often we think that the process is one of rote ceremony before meals, bedtime, or a sporting event. I believe in the power of prayer because my life has been changed through people praying for and over me. My hope is that you can say the same: that prayer matters to you because you've seen its power.

How often are you praying for your kids and mentees? Do you have a set time and place to do so? Is there a marker in your life that reminds you of this essential practice each day? It could be as obvious and simple as a "Pray for Lisa Today" Post It on the bathroom mirror. Is your mentee's birthday on October the sixth? Set an alarm to go off daily at 10:06am and spend one minute praying for him. Be as creative as you'd like to ensure consistency and commitment. You'll find the more you pray for your kids and mentees, the more you'll be asking them how you can be praying for them and that is a great encouragement.

The Giving Tree (Love is Sacrifice)

Shel Silverstein's poetry played a big role in my upbringing. Another reason why my sister and I loved spending time at Nardi's house was because she would take *A Light in the Attic* or *Where the Sidewalk Ends* from the shelf and read those quirky, smart, and hilarious poems to us with such inflection and fervor that we'd all laugh until our sides hurt.

One of Silverstein's books would become a mainstay in our home once Mandi and I started having children. It has been one of our favorites to read to our kids. *The Giving Tree* is a beautiful story of friendship and selflessness that everyone should know about and read. Having developed a skateboard graphic based on the book's cover, we get to tell the story often at skate camps and at the skate park when we give a board away to a skater. It's not only a beautiful story – it's the Gospel.

There is no substitute for reading that actual book, no matter how old you are, you'll enjoy it and certainly pick up on the metaphor. Here is a quick overview of the story:

There once was a tree and a little boy. They were best friends who would spend every day together. The boy spent hours swinging from the tree's branches and resting in its shade.

One day, the boy said he was hungry. So, the tree said,

"Here, boy, eat my apples" (ok, forgot to tell you it was an apple tree). The boy was happy because he was full, and the tree was happy because the boy was happy.

A few years down the road, the boy, who was getting older and more conscious of the competitive housing market, said, "I want to build a house." So, the tree said, "Here boy, cut down my branches and use the wood to make a house so you can have shelter and so that you can be happy." The boy climbed up into the tree, cut down its branches, and made a house with the boards. The boy was happy because he had a place to live. The tree was happy because the boy was happy.

Years passed and the "boy" had lived enough to know there's more to life than just the security of food and a mortgage. There was also adventure. So, he went to the tree, and he told it that he was tired of the rat race and the monotony. He said he wanted to build a boat and see the world.

Once again, the tree offered to freely give that which he had. "Come, boy," it said, "come and take my trunk. Build a boat and go see the world so you can be happy." The boy took a saw and cut down the rest of the tree, leaving only a stump where a mighty tree once stood. He hollowed out the massive trunk and made himself a boat. Then he brought it to the water's edge and sailed away from the tree to see the world and find adventure.

After many, many years, we find the tree alone and much shorter than in years past. The boy, who has lived many years and had many experiences returns to the tree who instantly recognizes him. The tree is very happy to see the boy, yet it apologizes for having no apples to feed the boy, no branches that the boy can use for shelter, and no trunk for the boy to use to find joy and excitement. In fact, the tree is only a stump now and is feeling useless.

The boy says he doesn't need food, shelter, or even adventure now that he's old and tired. All he really needs is a place to sit down. So, the tree rights itself as much as it can and says, "Come, boy, come and sit." And the story ends with the boy being happy to sit and the tree being happy because its friend had returned.

I'll admit that as I've read this story to three kids the past almost twenty years, I'm still unable to get through it without getting choked up and teary when speaking the words of the tree that gives, and gives, and then gives some more.

I also need to admit that I'm always bugged by the boy. He takes, and takes, and then takes some more.

It's clear why we at Middleman decided to use the cover of this story for what is by far our most popular skateboard graphic. While the tree is dropping an apple to the boy on the book cover, our graphic shows the tree handing the boy a skateboard (with the two Ms adorning the tree's trunk).

The world struggles to define and exercise true love. This children's book goes far in giving us a look at what it means to truly love someone. The tree didn't stop at expressing love by telling the boy how much it loved him. The tree didn't love the boy out of its renewable resources. Instead, the tree loved the boy sacrificially in a way that cost much and proved even more.

This is the type of love that God the Father exercised in sending and sacrificing Jesus the Son in place of our sin and for our ultimate good. How much does God love you? Enough to sacrifice perfection for you. He did this because He is good, and He can be trusted. Love is sacrifice.

Checks and Balances

As previously addressed in chapter four, Jesus told his friends before they left on their mission trip, they would have the power and opportunity to freely give because they had been freely given to by God in Matthew 10:7-8. This meant much more than not worrying about where their next meal was going to come from on the trip. He was giving them truth that was to inform the rest of their time together under His care as well as what life was going to look like after He died, and the Holy Spirit would come at Pentecost (Acts 2). In fact, the freely given so freely give logic would be preached and practiced for every generation after the disciples as a foundational truth of God's love and a Christian's heritage.

To best understand this principle, let's shine a light on the world's economics in relationships. In the absence of grace and mercy, we find a relational infrastructure consisting of checks and balances, currency, principles, and practices in place to keep the engine humming. How does one navigate a "successful" relationship in the absence of grace? It's simple really, just keep your eye on the scale.

A double-pan balance is the image most of us conjure in our minds when we think of a balanced scale. It is the scale we would see a granite statue of Justice holding atop a stereotypical courthouse. The scale type dates to 5000 BC and the word "balance" literally derives its meaning from the words "two pans." A balanced relationship is one that has equal giving and taking. When both partners in a marriage are equally meeting each other's needs by investing into the relationship, there is smooth sailing. Its only when one member of the agreement begins to slack off that the scales begin to tip and there is trouble in paradise.

When Jesus tells his friends they don't need to hold a scale of fairness up to every transaction they will experience on their trip, he's giving them the freedom from expectation that we often burden ourselves within relationships. Have you ever held back serving someone because she hasn't been serving you lately? Have you ever stopped yourself from giving someone something good because you convinced yourself he already has enough good things in his life? At the root of this type of relational decision making is selfishness, conditional love, and fear.

Jesus telling us that God has freely given to us so we can freely give to others tells us two theological and practical truths:

1)What God gives me I don't need from someone else

2) I will never run out of God's love so I can give it away indefinitely

God Freely Gives What Only He Can Give

God is the giver of identity and purpose. Since these things come from Him, I don't need to waste my time looking for them elsewhere. I haven't hurt myself very often in life. Even with the years of riding skateboards and motorcycles and working on some questionable projects I have been blessed to stay safe over the years. However, about twenty years ago, my good friend Zeek welded together and gifted me with some heavy-duty speaker stands. Before installing them in our living room, I discovered that each stand needed a hole drilled in the top and bottom plate so the speaker wires could run through, and each would have a cleaner look. So, one Friday afternoon I found myself standing in the garage in front of the three-foot-tall metal stand with a drill in hand. The job was simple – hold the drill over the top plate and pull down as the drill gets going and the hole is formed. What could go wrong? Well, the variable I hadn't considered was the stand's square sheet metal base that had some sharp edges and its four sharp corners. I also wasn't thinking about the worst-case scenario of the drill bit catching the entire speaker stand and turning it into a helicopter blade at my feet because I decided to do the job wearing flip flops. Well, guess what happened. That's correct. Within minutes I was driving to the ER for stitches and nearly lost a toe.

One of the important things we teach about safety in the shop at Middleman, and at home, is that most accidents occur when we attempt to use a tool for a job it wasn't designed for. Really hear this because it's done a lot. How many times are you needing to pull a rusty screw from its housing and instead of walking over to get a pry bar, you turn your socket wrench sideways and use it as a hammer? I rest my case. In the name of convenience and saving time, we often cut corners and compromise our safety by using the wrong tool for the job.

We do this in relationships too.

If my identity and purpose are to be found in God alone, why would I ever put that kind of burden on my wife, kids, career, talent, passions, etc.? Everything else besides God will buckle under the stress of that kind of pressure. Our spouses are the biggest target for this error. If I depend on Mandi to speak and exercise ultimate value into my life, she might do a good job of it. She, after all, is loving and selfless. She is considerate and humble. She is beautiful too. In fact, Mandi is the godliest person on earth that I've ever met. So how could I ever be left for wanting in this ideal marriage?

While Mandi is godly, she's not God.

She never will be. One of the huge successes of our relationship that has spanned over thirty years and our rich marriage that has been a joy for us over twenty years is that we understand that we are not each other's Messiahs. That spot is reserved for God Himself.

Ok, only God is God. But what does that mean in the real world and how does that fact inform my relationships? For one, I remember that I need to value my relationship with God. I need to pray. I need to read the Bible. I need to do things that help me remember that God is FOR me, and God is WITH me. I need to remember God is faithful even when I am not. I remember that God is perfect in the best kind of way. In contrast, I remember that even though there are some great people in my life who love me well, they are not God. They will make mistakes. They will take days off. They will forget me, and they will fail me. My pastor will do this as my friends will as my parents and even my wife will. But, if I stay connected to God through obedience, I am so much better at seeing the difference between what He can give me and what I should expect from everyone else in my life.

God's Love Never Ends and Never Runs Dry

In attempting to explain God's love to people in conversation or if I'm teaching somewhere I typically use two metaphors. One is the bank account, and one is the ocean. When Jesus was telling his friends to go out there and serve people, he wanted them to do so without the fear of limited resources. I think this is an area of spiritual growth that many struggle with today.

The world has never been smaller with social media and the speed at which news now travels. These days, I can be as worried about the water levels of Lake Waco less than a half mile away from my house as I can the speed of ice caps melting, oil quantities, and endangered animals in places I'll never visit. One of the greatest fears that millions of people suffer through every day is the general imbalance between supply and demand. Limited resources with an endless need for them will keep us awake at night and has been enough of a concern for many people to sit on years' worth of food and fuel while stockpiling generators and solar panels.

When you believe the only thing real in this world is what you can see, you will live with this fear on a moment-by-moment basis and do everything in your power to stretch resources to their fullest potential. Sadly, some take this approach to God's love. Just as I mentioned the two-plate scale, people will often limit the amount of love they are willing to exercise on someone out of fear they will run out of it. Again, Jesus said you have been freely given so you may now freely give.

It's like God has signed you up for a checking account and He's handed over a checkbook, (Oh geez, if you're unsure what a checkbook is maybe just put this book down now and google it) and He's told you that you can love people in such a way as it would be like going out and spending the rest of your time on this earth writing checks and handing them over to everyone you meet. But you'd say, wait, don't I need to balance the account after each transaction to make sure I don't overdraft and get penalized for insufficient funds?!

That's when God says, "Hey, don't apply your frugal way of thinking when it comes to My love. You can't write a hot check here. Just freely give. I have more in My account than you could ever spend over a lifetime."

Ok, I feel like my bank account metaphor is dated and

I'm not sure if I can relate it as well to something like Venmo so now I'll talk about the ocean.

Loving people feels like monitoring a faucet sometimes. Those of us who grew up with siblings can probably remember being served at the dining room table where we formed many of our standards of fairness and equality. One of the most obvious times was when we would pour glasses of juice or water. It was at those times when we learned how to get down at sea level as glasses were being poured to ensure that everyone was getting the exact SAME amount of juice. If the levels were off by one millimeter, we would demand what we were owed until justice was served.

The problem with delivering love with such a keen eye for equality is that it's like cutting people off at the spigot of our hearts because for some reason we are afraid that we will run out or that there won't be enough to make it until Friday based on where the water level is.

Jesus talked about water levels a few times in the Bible. We are so easily frightened about the idea of running out of electricity, fuel, toilet paper, hamburger meat, etc. Jesus told the woman at the well that people who partake of the Living Water never thirst again.

Imagine being able to serve others in such a way that you wouldn't be worried about how this is going to make you look. Imagine freely giving instead of convincing yourself that the person will probably use your dollar to buy drugs or that she probably has a car better than yours parked around the corner. Imagine loving in such a way that there's always another check ready to be written and an unlimited ocean connected to the other end of your spigot.

Freely you've been given. Freely give.

Reframing Circumstances with Terry Nelson

After a couple of years helping to plant a church in Austin, Mandi and I moved to Tomball, Tx to do youth ministry at Graceview Baptist. Besides nearly killing Phoebe and a girl named Summer, those years were some of the fullest and most rewarding for us. One youth worker and parent who mentored me during that time was a man named Terry Nelson. He was a good man who loved the Lord, his family, and the Church. One day Terry called and said that he'd like to start meeting with me before our Sunday morning small groups to pray and talk about things. I can remember immediately agreeing to the meet up but also thinking it was going to be yet another thing I would have to do early on a Sunday morning and my dance card was already full.

Little did I know those early morning meetings would be such a gift. After Terry would help me arrange chairs and place ping pong tables where they belonged, we'd sit down on the stage together and he'd ask me about my week. I remember telling him about a problem I was having once and he said, "Oh, that's not a problem, John. Cancer is a problem. What you're talking about is an opportunity!"

Now if I had a nickel for every time I've repeated Terry Nelson's wisdom to a person I could easily buy you dinner and a movie and would have plenty left over for popcorn.

Understanding that many of the "problems" we face are opportunities to learn new things and grow is a healthy way to live a life. It's certainly an indicator that you understand that our mindset should be stronger and more resilient than the power of circumstances which seek to undo us.

Yes is Yes and No is No

You know the kind of people who care about grammar, usage, and spelling to the point of correcting strangers on social media platforms? Yeah, I'm naturally one of those kinds of people. But I catch myself because I figure we only get one chance to communicate to someone for the first time so instead of writing them a ticket from the grammar police, I scroll on and simply shake my head in quiet disapproval and superiority.

From what I read, the advent of texting shorthand and emoji representation has placed spelling and grammar issues in the back seat for modern society. I'm hoping that won't drive the value of our words any farther down than they are now.

Jesus thought it was important enough while preaching to speak into the issue of folks making oaths and swearing by heaven and earth. He wasn't happy with it. His instruction on the matter was to understand that your Yes should be Yes and your No should be No and that was the end of it.

The strength of your word should be enough. If you say you're going to do something, you do it. There is no reason to promise or swear or make an elaborate oath on the matter to give yourself more weight or substance. When our word has lost its power due to our going back on it, we begin to lose a bit of ourselves in a bad way. When Bilbo Baggins considers the ring's toll on his spirit, he says he feels "all thin, sort of stretched, if you know what I mean: like butter that has been scraped over too much bread."

Devaluing our word creates a fraying of our integrity that others must endure and that we must work hard to come back from. There were times a parent or a church member came to me with an issue and mentioned how many other people shared the same concern. This was seldom the truth, but we sometimes lack confidence in our own word and our personal position on a matter to feel comfortable voicing an issue from our singular perspective.

How do you value your word enough so you can lead with integrity and then be free to help your children or mentees replicate your success? Start right now by simply saying what you mean and meaning what you say. Don't let your mouth write checks that your (schedule) can't cash. If you shake a man's hand in agreement over a deal, realize you're locked into it and honor it. Let your Yes be Yes and your No be No.

The character Baba, from the book-turned-movie, *The Kite Runner*, teaches his son, Amir, that "there is only one sin. Only one. And that is theft, every other sin is a variant of theft." He goes on to explain that if you kill someone you are stealing that person's right to live his life and you are also stealing the opportunity of his loved ones to enjoy him in their lives.

When we lie, no matter how harmless or careless, we steal the right from others to the truth. We also steal integrity from ourselves.

As you may already know, integrity is the strength of character that all people can nurture by living truthfully. Many will describe this attribute as who you are when no one else is looking. Our integrity should be of great value to us. We should put the hard work in of protecting it daily. It starts with valuing our words and making sure they line up with our actions. This is a natural process of one who understands their truest identity and fleshes it out by living with intentional purpose.

When those values are prioritized at our heart level, we can encourage our kids and mentees to follow our examples. We sometimes minimize the importance of integrity by allowing small circumstances to get by us and instead focus on the more important matters of moral living. But the cost of our integrity is always in direct proportion to what we're willing to trade for it.

Steal a million dollars? You traded your integrity for that amount.

Steal one dollar? That is the exact price you're willing to pay to have your integrity compromised.

Let's try holding our integrity to a higher standard. Doing this hard work will pay off when you realize we, as parents and mentors, are constantly being watched and studied by people trying to figure out what being an adult looks like and what the true value of our words are.

Feast or Famine, Thick or Thin, a Deal's a Deal, Sink or Swim

From the early days of maritime tattooing, sailors have cut inked images into their skin that represent their lives at sea. Designs have included faraway loved ones, everyday duties, nautical triumphs, and superstitions that surround life on the seven seas.

The popular "Hold Fast" tattoo written across a sailor's knuckles indicate their careers as deckhands. It's said that having Hold Fast on each of a sailor's hands granted them luck and the grip they needed to weather storms and work with the ship's lines and rigging.

The tattoo could also serve to remind married people of

the agreement they made to each other when they stood in front of friends and family and committed to hold fast to one another come what may.

I was shocked one Wednesday night at youth group when our youth minister, Troy, led a Bible study over the topics of love and relationships. He told the room full of teenagers that he didn't always "feel" love for his wife, Kelley. Scandalous. He was trying to tell us that the bond of the relationship was far stronger, deeper, and more consistent than what mere emotions can offer.

That's what makes a covenant so valuable. It is an agreement, or contract, between two people that says no matter how we feel about it later, we will hold fast to one another and endure circumstances.

Mandi jokingly told me last night, "My only regret in all of this is that we didn't move to California right after getting married." Mind you, this statement wasn't made within the context of a larger conversation. I had just walked into the room where she was so I could take my socks off. (But this, my friend, is one of the countless little beautiful things that I love about the woman.) We talked a little more about it and it was easy to remember that when we got married, we were incredibly excited, but we were also cautiously optimistic based on our both having divorced parents.

If we were to get married today, I'm sure we would move to California right away (I'd take California in 1999 over the California of 2022. Ok, actually, give me California in the early 70s. We could move into the apartment complex where Glenn Frey and Don Henley have talked about living on the second floor over a young songwriter named Jackson Browne. Those guys got to hear "Doctor My Eyes" being written every morning as the newly formed verses and choruses wafted up through the floor off Jackson's piano.)

The truth is, Mandi and I didn't have the margin to consider taking such a leap when we were newlyweds. We wanted to do everything we could to ensure the health of a relationship which would look different from the ones we witnessed growing up. Things may have looked different for us had we examples of adventurous couples who were dreamers spurring us on to head out west, but the first five years of our marriage were a gift which included storms weathered and valuable lessons learned. As Mandi says, within our dating years and early in marriage we were "two kids raising each other."

When I get the chance to officiate a couple's wedding ceremony, I like to share the secret of my marriage's success during meetings prior to the ceremony. Every morning when I wake up, I look over at Mandi and I remind myself of a simple truth: I don't deserve her. I am not saying she is perfect or any more virtuous than she is. I am saying that even with all the work that it takes and how inefficient and inconvenient the marriage relationship can be, it is only by God's grace that I would have someone as beautiful and selfless and intelligent and graceful and considerate and intentional and kind ever agree to marry someone like me.

Then again, a deal's a deal.

CHAPTER 11

WAITING FOR MY REAL LIFE TO BEGIN

(Peace)

Any minute now, my ship is coming in
I'll keep checking the horizon
I'll stand on the bow
Feel the waves come crashing
Come crashing down, down, down, on me
And you say, be still my love
Open up your heart
Let the light shine in
But don't you understand
I already have a plan
I'm waiting for my real life to begin
-from Colin Hay's "Waiting for My Real Life to Begin"

WITH > FOR

Sometimes I'll get a call from a school administrator or a pastor who is looking for a skate team to come do a demo for kids. BTW a "demo" is a demonstration which skateboard companies have provided for skate shops over the years. The idea is that a traveling group of professional or amateur skateboarders will meet up in a shop's parking lot to skate for the crowd and then hold an autograph session in the shop to boost a shop's sales. You can imagine that the best demos are those which showcase the best skaters and the biggest names.

Even at my peak of ability and impressiveness, my skills and showmanship were not enough to initiate or maintain a crowd's interest.

Sometimes professional skaters become Christians and then they can leverage their abilities and/or name to draw local skaters to events and demos so they can share their faith and invite others to follow Jesus. This kind of ministry is invaluable for reaching many people for Jesus. I love that God uses talented skaters with noteworthy names to tell more people about His love for them.

But it ain't me babe. No, no, no, it ain't me babe. It ain't me you're looking for babe. (If you read that line in the voice of Bob Dylan or Johnny Cash, I can tell that we are gonna be friends.)

That's not our philosophy at Middleman and it's not our method. We also believe that skating with kids is a lot more fun than skating for them.

In the Old Testament (1 Sam 12-15), King Saul was told to wipe out the Amalekites. He was instructed by God to kill comprehensively and completely everybody. Destroy their warriors, all the men, all the women, all the children, and all their animals. It was God's plan to put a 100% end to the Amalekite people. But somewhere along the way, Saul thought he had a better idea. He figured he would neutralize the threat by killing off the warriors but allow the king and the valuable livestock of the land to live. The Bible says he then thought he did such a good job that he even set up a monument for himself. So, then Samuel the prophet (who was pulling for Saul by praying for him through the night) goes to see Saul in his anguish. Saul unsuccessfully defended his misguided reasoning to Samuel by saying his plan was to "sacrifice" all these valuable things to the Lord. Samuel had enough and just said, "Stop!" He goes onto tell him that there is a huge difference between coming up with our own ideas about what will please the Lord and simple obedience. Samuel tells Saul (and us today) that "obedience is better than sacrifice."

Doing things WITH God is always a better decision than doing things FOR Him.

So, what does this mean for the ministry you run, the family you are a part of, and even the small decisions you make daily? The same thing it meant for Saul. What does God require? Simple obedience and nothing less: With > For.

The Bible tells us that Mephibosheth's life became fuller after having his identity realized, his purpose experienced, and his community invested in. He goes on to get married and have children of his own. Isn't it interesting that healthy community breeds more of the same?

Peace is Where Identity, Purpose, and Community find their Fulfilment and Rest

In a unique place in scripture, Jesus sends an invitation to those who need him as he defines and describes himself:

> *"Come to me, all who labor and are heavy laden, and I will give you rest. Take my yoke upon you and learn from me; for I am gentle and lowly in heart, and you will find rest for your souls. For my yoke is easy, and my burden is light." Matt 11:28-30*

What an efficiency of words within three verses. He beckons the overwhelmed to come, take, learn, and find. He says he will give, teach, and comfort. He does these things because He is gentle and lowly in heart. In Him, we can be a seated soul because he is a rest giver with an easy yoke and a light burden. Jesus's being "lowly in heart" speaks as much to his humility as it does his accessibility.

How Do You Make the Board Jump Like That?

These days, even non-skaters know that the ollie is the foundational maneuver that most skate tricks are built on. Before it's invention, skaters would do bonelesses, bunny hop their boards, and even "gorilla grabs" which included gripping the board at the front and back with their bare toes and jumping with it. Man, I'm glad those days are over. Vert skater Alan "Ollie" Gelfand is credited for inventing the ollie in the mid 70s. Freestyle and street virtuoso Rodney Mullen adapted it to flat ground in the early 80s and thus helped define what skateboarding would look like from then on. Growing up, I was most influenced by pro skaters Natas Kaupas and Ron Allen as they took ollies to the next level in height and style.

During the 80s, if you saw a kid wearing a skate shirt, you'd ask him if he skated. If he said "yes," the next question might be "how high can you ollie?" Clearly, the ollie was a litmus test of ranking that would indicate how long you have been skating and how good you really were.

The trick is based on a combination of moves which involves jumping, which gives you height, and popping the tail, which keeps the board "attached" to your feet. Ollie mechanics are simple to explain and understand yet difficult for many to apply right away as it is a learned process of timing and control. I typically tell new skaters to allot 300 attempts before they will land a decent ollie.

Before we were old enough for driver's licenses, we South Houston street rats would hop the Metro bus on a Saturday morning and make our way up I-45 to skate downtown Houston. It took forever to get there. But there were many adventures to enjoy with the characters who assembled on the bus. Downtown offered a skate terrain unlike anywhere else we skated at the time. Riding in the neighborhood or skating to parking lots meant a lot of stopping, picking up our boards, and walking to the next decent piece of concrete. But downtown was a limitless concrete jungle of expansive beautifully poured asphalt streets and wide concrete sidewalks that connected commercial-grade granite courtyards, limestone benches, and marble fountains as far as the eye could see.

The only issue I experienced over the first couple of times I skated downtown was that of not yet being able to ollie high enough or with enough confidence to skate seamlessly from street level up to the curb without clunkingly skidding on a foot, stopping my skateboard, picking it up, and placing it on the sidewalk before pushing once more. The stop and go nature of this process was confining.

But then one day it happened.

I knew I could do it, all I needed was to overcome the mental block trying to convince me otherwise. We had been skating for at least an hour so far, moving from one building to the next, staying just long enough to get a few tricks in before we succumbed to the angry men with mustaches in navy blazers and walkie-talkies yelling at us to leave. We rode as a pack toward One Shell Plaza much like the dangerous and misunderstood Daggers from *Thrashin'*. I watched some who led the group ollie cleanly up the curb and onto the sidewalk without a thought or strain of effort. Some even rode a manual for a car length or pulled a frontside 180 before turning back around to further propel themselves with Airwalks and Vision Street Wear slapping the pavement.

And then, I go for it. Roll, roll, roll. Pop! (Oh, the quiet and reverent millisecond between an ollie's Genesis and Revelation. A beautiful sound, indeed.) Roll, roll, roll.

Success!

I'm on the sidewalk. I look back at the defeated curb and the trailing stampede of skaters behind me. I begin stacking the symbolic stones of memorial for such a time as this in my mind. It was more than just an eight-inch display of centrifugal force; it was a breakthrough. The overcoming of fear with locked-in commitment fused to form euphoric liberation.

From that moment on, downtown Houston no longer sat as a restrictive grid of confining concrete squares requiring a predictable and unnatural stop, lift, drop, and go movement. It was now a free roam environment that brought with it an odd sense of peace.

It was the difference between going over to play side-scrolling games on Chuck Powell's NES in seventh grade every morning before school and experiencing the go anywhere and do anything of Mario 64 on the Nintendo 64 while in college nearly ten years later. Freedom!

The real fruit of a defined identity, clear purpose, and healthy community is as liberating as it is peaceful. I believe it to be what many of us hope for, but fewer have experienced.

How many of us are waiting for the peace to come that should follow living as who we truly are, doing what we really need to be doing during the limited time we are here, and spending our days investing in and being invested in by our community? If that kind of peace and freedom are not real in our lives perhaps it's due to a lack of correct IPC.

IPC vs CPI

King David's life shows us the natural IPC progression. He knew who he was (Identity), knew what to do based on it (Purpose), and related to others to accomplish it (Community). Once he applied these values to his daily life, he modelled and freely offered them to Mephibosheth. That high level of self-realization and consideration for others resulted in a peaceful mindset and peaceful living.

Why don't we see this model used more often in our various social networks?

Throughout their lives, most people interact with highly defined groups and organizations that have needs. For example, a football team is comprised of athletes of different sizes and abilities based on their positions. To keep an opposing team's receiver from making a catch and scoring a touchdown, a football team needs a defensive player called a safety who can run fast, jump high, and keep up with the receiver on that opposing team. So, the COMMUNITY of the team sets to find a skillset based on a required PURPOSE and then drafts a player who fits the IDENTITY of a good safety (CPI which is in direct opposition of the IPC progression).

What's wrong with this model?

If both purpose and identity of an individual are dictated solely by a community's needs, the individual has no choice but to suffer rejection when the community decides it no longer needs his services. In every area of life, one's purpose is all too often confused for identity. The financial guru causes his company to lose money and so, he gets fired. The wife is no longer desired by her husband and so, she suffers a divorce. The football player's knee fails, he gets cut from the team (see *Friday Night Lights* the movie. But then watch the show too. Texas Forever.)

CPI never results in peace and rest. It can't. It's performance-based and performance-based social hierarchies utilize competition and fear to draw results out of the individual that will best serve the community. Don't like it? There are ten other people behind you who would love to have your spot. Even churches can take on the CPI approach when led by ego-driven pastors or power-hungry committees.

An Instrument of Thy Peace

Lord, make me an instrument of Thy peace:
where there is hatred, let me sow love
where there is injury, pardon
where there is doubt, faith
where there is despair, hope

where there is darkness, light
where there is sadness, joy.
O divine Master, grant that I may not so much seek
to be consoled as to console,
to be understood as to understand,
to be loved as to love.
For it is in giving that we receive,
it is in pardoning that we are pardoned,
and it is in dying that we are born to eternal life.
Amen.

At the time of this writing, the newest graphic at Middleman is what we call the "Instrument" design. My friend, Cory Romieser, took just about as long designing it as he did for the "Freely We Give" graphic. It seemed to design itself. My only direction for the piece was that it featured the specific text surrounded by flora and fauna. I was excited about the Instrument graphic because it gives the wearer of our t-shirt or hoodie the chance to be mindful in communicating the message written across their back. Wearing the message means we prayerfully go about our day hoping to be just that – God's instrument that He uses to make things as peaceful on earth as they are in heaven. The same goes for our skateboard graphic with the same message. It may be a stretch for some, but we like the idea that a skateboard can be considered a tool God uses for His purpose (as well as a weapon of mass destruction on red curbs).

How would you define peace? It's a question I always ask teenagers. Because our brains often function through a balanced dichotomy of opposites to understand and distinguish between things, the most common answer I hear is "peace is the absence of war." While the presence of peace may result in the end of conflict, that less-than-optimal answer may hold more for us to understand why and how we can experience peace even during conflict, inconvenience, and hurt.

A better understanding of peace starts by considering the presence of coordinated existence. Have you ever seen footage of tightly drawn schooling fish in the ocean? It's impressive to see hundreds of fish moving as one mass in the salt water. They do this for several reasons. When fish school, it increases their swimming efficiency and helps to conserve energy. This can keep the community (or school) safer while traveling from one reef to the next. They may also school as it brings the sexes together and makes for easier reproduction (geez guys, get a room, I'm swimming here). Some schools are even formed by all-female members to help keep harassing male fish at bay.

Some communities have such a low tolerance for any kind of individual formation or expression that their gate of acceptance is very narrow and guarded closely to insure those allowed in look like us, talk like us, and act like us.

Paul spoke into this issue when the young church in Corinth struggled to operate peacefully, using our physical bodies as the metaphor: "*The eye cannot say to the hand, "I have no need of you," nor again the head to the feet, "I have no need of you." On the contrary, the parts of the body that seem to be weaker are indispensable, and on those parts of the body that we think less honorable we bestow the greater honor, and our unpresentable parts are treated with greater modesty, which our more presentable parts do not require. But God has so composed the body, giving greater honor to the part that lacked it, that there may be no division in the body, but that the members may have the same care for one another. If one member suffers, all suffer together; if one member is honored, all rejoice together."* 1 Cor 12

One thing we love about ministering to a lot of kids who don't spend most of their time in organized sports is that the teenagers who are skaters, artists, and musicians will grow up to be our voices. They will be the ones writing songs that we as mainstream folks will connect with and sing along to. They'll make movies we go to see and write poetry that expresses our feelings because we don't have the words. For years, art and music programs have taken a hit in public education because they're often not bottom-line friendly. The truth is that creative endeavors in all their countless forms bring us closer to God and to each other.

Living peacefully has very little to do with extinguishing all forms of conflict from our lives. In fact, many of our most-peaceful leaders and servants operate within communities plagued by conflict and violence. This is true of historical leaders like Gandhi and Mother Teresa as well as contemporary peacemaker and Homeboy Industries leader, Father Greg Boyle. His story of equipping and encouraging former gang members and the incarcerated in east Los Angeles in the name of the Lord is inspiring. Boyle's "Tattoos on the Heart" is an excellent read that reminds us that a key ministry ingredient is remembering that those we serve minister to us just as much as we minister to them. In failing to remember this we run the risk of confusing glories and it can hinder us further in developing a heart of peace.

> *"May the God of hope fill you with all joy and peace as you trust in him, so that you may overflow with hope by the power of the Holy Spirit." Romans 15:13*

CHAPTER 12

KIND AND GENEROUS

(Gratitude)

Oh, I want to thank you for so many gifts you gave The love, the tenderness, I want to thank you I want to thank you for your generosity, the love And the honesty that you gave me I want to thank you show my gratitude
-from Natalie Merchant's "Kind and Generous"

Mandi and I walked through the sleepy coastal village in Ireland and sat down to have a hard conversation. We'd been married five years and were trying to start our family and it wasn't automatic. We sat shoulder to shoulder looking out near the cliffs watching the boats slowly and quietly pass in and out of the bay. We breathed in the salty air and talked about our options, whether we would try alternative methods to get pregnant or get testing done. The topic of adoption was discussed as well and I can remember us getting up from our talk with the resolve that whatever we do, we'll do it together and however we grow our family, it's sure to be a blessing. Then we went back to the Mermaid Pub because the tuna melts were so good.

Nine months after returning from vacation, Mandi had our first daughter, and we named her Dylin Rachel. I'm happy to say we kept the lights on and everybody fed after Mandi quit her job and began staying home to raise our kids full-time. We took to heart the conversation we had just a few years earlier with a woman who hosted a youth retreat group Mandi and I co-led as newlyweds. I can't remember the woman's name, but I do remember standing in her yard and leaning on a pecan tree as she worked a flowerbed on her hands and knees and shared some of her family's story. She and her husband were now empty nesters and she asked what our plans were once we started having kids. Her advice: "Even if you have to eat beans every night for supper, you should if that's what it takes for you to raise your kids. Spend as much time with them as you can." The advice she gave that day was a comfort to us as Mandi wanted to homeschool and, eventually, so did I.

Transitioning from a dual-income family to a single-income home after having children was no simple task. While my dad covered my first semester's tuition, I worked through my entire undergraduate education and graduated with zero debt. We paid off all of Mandi's residual student loans over the first few years of our marriage. We paid off cars as well and lived frugally. But the old line of "you spend what you make" always seems to be true. Having our income cut in half with expenses only increasing (newsflash, kids are expensive) led us to consider our options at the time.

Part of the issue dealt with my paycheck. Making the move from a church plant to an established church meant a greater sense of income security. Working for a church isn't much different than working for any kind of business out there in that all hired positions include job descriptions, salary packages, and benefits. As working for Graceview was my first real church gig that included dealing with a pastor, executive staff members, and committees you can see how the waters of communication, interpretation, accountability, and decision-making can get muddy. That isn't to say I was blatantly abused, misled, or lied to. In fact, I was kept from much of the harm and betrayal that many of my colleagues endure throughout my twenty-year tenure as a church leader.

As things were getting financially tighter at home, I met with the church's personnel committee so they could be made aware of the issue and see if there were any solutions we could find together. The one card I had to play in the meeting was a conversation I had with the executive pastor during the hiring process in which he said that even though I'm starting out at humble beginnings, once I serve for some time on staff, I'll see my income increase.

I'll liken this arrangement to the one in *Rudy* where Sean Astin's character goes to the new coach of Notre Dame football and tells him about the arrangement he had with the previous coach that included his suiting up for a game. Even if you haven't seen the movie, you have a fair idea of how valuable that card I had to play was.

After I shared my issue with the finance committee, I was told my request would be denied but that I could have made a stronger case for myself if I was more like another staff member who constantly displays a sense of urgency and frantic busyness whenever committee members visit the church office during the week. By this, I learned that some folks who gauge our worth can interpret what they called "running around the office like a chicken with her head cut off" as a high degree of nervous energy that results in financial compensation. It flew in the face of the leadership approach I practice which values preparedness and pacing that feels and looks a lot less frantic. In other words, "you're making it look too easy so you must not be doing enough." One more note to those in church leadership: beware of financial decision makers who consider a salary as compensation for unhealthy environments instead of reward for a job well-done. You shouldn't make more only after becoming more miserable.

The issue was finalized with my pastors' relevant words he spoke while leaning back in his office chair looking at the ceiling tiles, "John, the truth is, if you don't get it during the hiring process, you usually don't ever get it." Amen. I've repeated these words a time or two to green-horn church leaders.

While that was a disappointing time for myself and our young family, it served as a mental turning point which hinged on a sticker Mandi applied to the top left corner of the refrigerator door. Four simple words written in blue on a white background: "Enough is a Banquet"

That time in our lives coincided with a discovery Mandi made about her health. For much of her life, she had eaten the traditional American diet which, in her case, included countless foot-long hot dogs from Sonic. Our being in youth ministry included years of Wednesday night pizzas and many meals that prioritized quantity over quality.

While we realized the need for healthy eating, it seemed ironic that we were becoming less and less able to afford everything in life, much less, organic fruits and vegetables. We would need to settle for those beans every meal after all!

The Lord then provided in an incredible way the day a box of fresh vegetables arrived at our door. It was from someone we hardly knew at church but felt directed to give to our family in that way. Soon after, our new friends, the Deerings, doubled their CSA order each pick up day and shared half their take with us. Mandi had just begun praying over the issue of how to eat well with dwindling resources. It filled our spirits and our stomachs.

Todd and Debbie Deering became great friends to us even helping us as we went from selling our home and moving into their guest house on their property. We didn't know it at the time, but the move would prove instrumental into our transitioning from Tomball to Brenham to live and serve there for six years.

Understanding that "enough is a banquet" means living with the trust and perspective that our having enough is quite more than enough.

The Top Three Gratitude Thieves

Limitations

As a people who can usually get anything we want any time we want it, we don't do well with hearing "no." How many times have you resented the good folks at Chick Fil A when you roll up to the empty parking lot only to remember that it's Sunday and you won't be enjoying your Jesus sandwich after all? I think we Texans have an even tougher time with limitations because we're just dying for someone to tell us we can't do a thing so we can show them that we sure will be doing that thing and we're gonna do that thing bigger and better than it's ever been done, bang bang! (Those are obviously six shooters being fired off in the sky, twirled, and then slipped back into holsters.)

We're so affected by limitations that we become upset when we can't have things we didn't even want in the first place. Sometimes we only want a thing because we can't have it. How many times have we been upset when a friend gets invited to a party by another friend we can't stand? Do we like the person throwing the party? No way. Would we have shown up at their house had we been invited? Again, not a chance. Are we offended that they didn't invite us? You bet we are and we're burning with righteous rage over here!

Fear

Just as fear puts the brakes on action, it can be a relentless thief of gratitude. Sometimes the simple love we have for our family or our lifestyle can create a fear in us that we might lose it all at the hands of a politician, immigrant, or the media. So instead of being free to be grateful, we're shackled and deathly afraid of losing the very things we're supposed to enjoy. A good remedy for this mindset is to own all things openhandedly. My friends, Tod and Seanna, are really good at this one. They have some cool stuff because they live on land and have raised three fun kids. I like to tell people when they see our cool stuff, that "our stuff is your stuff." I think I got that from Tod.

Comparison

Comparison is also one of life's greatest gratitude thieves. It seems our possessions and accomplishments can never be good enough when we know someone who has better stuff than we do. The practice of "keeping up with the Joneses" for many folks living in the suburbs keeps us in a constant state of acquiring the latest and greatest toys, cars, and houses. Throwing our kids into the mix takes it to another level. I saw a commercial for a supplement drink marketed for kids that showed a disappointed parent realizing his son was shorter than other kids in his class. The solution? Billy needs to start chugging these over-engineered and vitamin-laced chocolate smoothies or he will never measure up to the taller kids. But literally. Because he's shorter than the other kids. Ugh again.

What's the antidote for the poison of limitations, fear, and comparison? Just as these three issues are detrimental to a healthy mindset, intentionally practicing gratitude counteracts them. Are you thankful for what you have? Then, take care of what you have. Stephen Stills said it best, "If you can't be with the one you love, honey, love the one you're with." Work to maintain relationships by investing time and effort into them. Spend energy caring for your possessions properly and they will last longer. The grass can be greener on your side when you commit to watering it.

A Word to Those Somebodies from Somewhere

I have wondered if my perspective on matters of God's grace and mercy are greatly affected by who I am and where I'm from. In other words, I feel greatly blessed by God in many ways because the life I now live is of far greater worth and weight than my expectations for what it would amount to over the first half of my life. I did not expect to have an incredible marriage, a healthy family, a career of service, and such enjoyable days. For the first twenty years of my life, I was a white boy in South Houston with no redeeming qualities who lived to ride a skateboard and had a hard time staying out of trouble. The next thirty years of my life looked drastically different as I spent them investing in others and being greatly invested into by others.

But maybe you were raised in a wealthy and stable family by parents who loved each other and instilled values into you that bred confidence in your future life choices. Maybe going to a respected and expensive college was a given for you. Maybe you were expected to start a fruitful career, marry well, and purchase a house worth more than the one you were raised in. Ministering to skaters and folks who lack some of life's essentials is easy. If I want to have a conversation with someone about Jesus being Living Water, I can start by giving the guy an actual bottle of water.

But what about addressing someone's identity, purpose, and community if their lives already look more like David's where victories and praises abound and less like Mephibosheth's hobbling around while calling himself a dead dog?

The short answer is that you don't have to be a nobody from nowhere to understand that this world has nothing to offer in the form of salvation (much less, identity, purpose, and community). People of means are sometimes the first to realize this fact because they don't have to romanticize about what it would mean to have the comforts of the world. They have them. And while they might enjoy them, they also realize that just as the Sabbath was made for man and not the other way around, so wealth is a tool for good and not the end result of a life well spent (Mark 8:36).

If your life has been marked by struggle and conflict because those who should have loved you well were abusive with unattainable expectations, conditional love, resentment for underachieving, or any other types and shapes of ugliness, I am sorry for that. I hope you will rest in the Lord's definition and application of identity, purpose, and community as well.

The Davids who Yelled "Mephibosheth!"

I am extremely grateful for the many Davids throughout my almost 50 years of life who yelled out my name in the midst of life's urgent demands and many distractions. It has been these people of margin who have, time and time again, shown me God's grace and have spoken louder than the inner voices of doubt telling me that I can't or that I shouldn't because I'm a nobody from nowhere.

I'm thankful to my parents, John and Janis and Kathy and Armando for keeping me fed, clothed, and housed. I am grateful for their having music readily available in the home during my childhood. In 1982, I snatched two cassette tapes, Eric Clapton's *Slowhand* and ZZ Top's *Dequello*, from the glovebox of Mando's 65 Chevy pickup and wore both tapes down thin, listening to them repeatedly. Speaking of petty theft, I apologize to Janis for so many years ago taking and never returning her Jayhawks and Tracy Chapman tapes from the living room entertainment stand drawer. Zeek probably still has them. I credit my mom for my enjoying singer songwriters of the 70s like Jim Croce, John Denver, Jackson Browne, and Gordon Lightfoot. I have vivid memories of travelling down the road and staring out of the back glass of her silver Buick Opel while listening to Juice Newton's card game lament over misguided love, Carly Simon recognizing vanity, and especially connecting with Linda Ronstadt because I too, as a five-year-old, must have been cheated and mistreated enough to wonder when will I be loved?

I had no idea that music would serve its purpose so well in connecting my young brain to concepts and imagery within chord progressions, verses, choruses, guitar solos, harmonies, music videos, live shows, album covers, liner notes, dissonance, and finally, resolution. I have always liked that so many songs begin on a major note, take a journey, and then end on that original note. It is an appropriate metaphor for us all as we leave home, enjoy and endure the love and loss of life, only to return back to where we started but as a fuller and wiser person.

My journey from home so far has included many more David-like mentors who have invested richly into my life. They have often been found in the Church and I owe a great deal of gratitude to staff members and folks who made up the congregations of Park Place Baptist, Highland Baptist, Rosebud Baptist, Lake Heights Church, Graceview Baptist, FBC Brenham, First Bellville, Harris Creek, and First Waco. Being a part of these churches throughout my faith journey has brought me closer to the Lord, gave me my Mandi, allowed me to meet some of my best friends, and sustained my family. Many of Middleman's team members are active members of these churches today.

There are so many examples of how folks have blessed me that I've forgotten more than I can remember. They have endured to form an incredible amount of gratitude in my heart, and I hope it will continue to increase my boldness for living out a life marked by peace and gratitude. To be so firmly planted on these realities should always result in confidently investing in others. That is why we turned a corner several years ago at Middleman by de-emphasizing our growth and championing other skate ministries.

We have worked with an incredible group of Middleman Mentors over the years including Lawton, Gabriel, Donnie, Micah, Peyton, Sam, and Ralph. These guys have done excellent work by sharing their faith with many and investing in the lives of teenagers where they live. Often when we meet skaters who want to serve their communities for Jesus, we discover they want to grow a creative ministry with names and logos and graphics and equipment. Once we realized we were more interested in building "The Kingdom" as opposed to a Middleman kingdom, we went all in with investing in skate ministries of all shapes and sizes needing nothing in return. So, whether we invest funds into another group's event, show up to serve coffee or shaved ice at a skate competition, or give a van away to a skate ministry, we are confident we will never lack for funds or resources. We truly believe that freely we have been given so...you know the rest by now.

Talk About the Mephibosheths

After sharing the first draft of this work with my editor, one of her notes included my need to share more stories of the Mephibosheths that I have invested in over the years. I know hearing the stories of how the teenagers I have known and invested in for two decades while leading in the church and through Middleman could help to connect the dots and reveal how I grew from a Mephibosheth into a David. I'm thankful for the opportunity to invest in others. It has been a joy to see many teenagers commit their lives to the Lord. But part of freely giving is not leveraging kindness for the sake of promotion.

This is perhaps no trickier than when handing a new

skateboard deck to someone at the park. There is always the temptation to ask the kid to "hold up the board so I can get a pic." More times than not I pass on taking the photo and posting it on social media. While it would afford me the chance to show donors how their support is being used in the community, it also nullifies the "freely we give" component of who we are. Giving something away "for free" while asking for something in return isn't so free.

In Matthew chapter six, Jesus spoke directly into the issue of how quickly we seek glory in the matters of giving to the needy, praying, and exercising the spiritual discipline of fasting. He warns us against "practicing your righteousness in front of others to be seen by them." Give in secret. Go into your room and close the door before praying. Fast without telling everybody how you're seeking God's direction through the pious self-denial of French fries today.

This is a lesson we can all take to heart as we live in an age when many produce content through social media yet few have anything original, substantial, inspiring, or encouraging to share. Perhaps there could be a return to holding some life experiences sacred or at least privileged.

Another way I know I am old-fashioned is that when I proposed to Mandi, I did so in private so the moment would be exclusively for the two of us. The moment forever lives in just her and my memory and the only physical memento from the day is a small, framed apple blossom picked from a tree that sits in our bedroom. The flower holds no significance for anyone in the world but me and my wife.

In contrast, many young couples today choose to document their proposals through a friend's recording of it through a phone. At the root of recorded events like proposals, gender-reveal parties, and taking photos of your desk as you are reading your Bible or eating a meal is the deep-seated desire to connect with others through encouraging community. There is nothing inherently wrong with that stance as we are right to celebrate together.

But imagine returning to the notion that there are times in life that exist just for the moment and exclusively for those physically near you. Jesus warns us that besides confusing glories we are also prone to miss out on what we should hear and see and think at times of great significance when we spend self-conscious energy attempting to curate a moment that has the potential to receive hundreds of views by strangers on their phones. Imagine being so grateful for moments between only you and your spouse that you plan them regularly and enjoy them exclusively.

Happy Trails

I hope time in this book has felt worth it. I hope you agree with some things I've said. I hope you disagree with some things. How else would you realize you've either got a lesson to learn from your being wrong or that I just proved myself human from my being wrong? I hope you have been equipped with a few more tools in your toolbox as well as encouraged to keep fighting the good fight on behalf of how God feels about you and how He feels about the folks you are investing in.

The Ragamuffin, Brennan Manning once said that he doesn't think that we'll be asked if we believed in or loved Jesus when we die and stand at heaven's gates. He said, instead, he thinks we'll be asked if we believe that Jesus loved us.

Even though King David was known as a man after God's

own heart, I think he knew that God was after his too.

That's how the world's Davids live and that's what the world's Mephibosheths need so they can become a little more like David themselves someday.

When Identity is realized,
Purpose is experienced,
Community is shared,
Peace is discovered,
and Gratitude overflows.

May God's glory overflow from our hearts as we stand before Him, look across the room at His beloved, and yell, "Mephibosheth!"

I find it only fitting to end this tale of relational investment by presenting a grainy shot of 17-year old me jumping a Toyota in a Dallas parking lot with one of my mentors looking on. Yes, that's Troy Sikes leaning on the car, sporting a killer 1991 mustache, khaki shorts, and ankle socks. This was the first ministry event I ever experienced that involved skateboarding and he was responsible for organizing and overseeing it. I am so grateful for the countless hours he spent tilling the soil, mining the gems, and guiding me through my formative years.

Thanks, Troy.

Long may you run.

ABOUT THE AUTHOR

John Barnard was born and raised in South Houston, Texas. Shortly after receiving his undergrad from Texas Tech, he began a twenty-year career in ministry which included roles as associate pastor, worship pastor, and youth minister in Lubbock, Austin, Houston, and rural Texas. He completed a master's in church leadership in 2012.

In 2005, John started mentoring skateboarders by building relationships, sharing his faith, and producing and giving away skateboards. Seven years later, he established Middleman Skateboard Ministries as a board-run nonprofit.

John and his wife, Mandi, moved their family to Waco to run Middleman as a full-time mentoring ministry in 2016. Today, Middleman focuses its efforts on local mentoring and supporting other skate ministries across the country by offering free resources, strategy, counseling, and financial support.

To find out more about Middleman or to contact John:

middleman-ministries.org

@middlemanskateboards

www.ingramcontent.com/pod-product-compliance
Lightning Source LLC
LaVergne TN
LVHW091143080826
845145LV00008B/2243

* 9 7 8 1 9 5 5 5 4 6 3 1 7 *